# Homeless by Choice

A Memoir of Love, Hate, and Forgiveness

Roy Juarez Jr.

Printed in the United States of America

First Printing, 2018

ISBN 978-1-7325507-8-0

IMPACTmemoirs Publishing
P.O. Box 27311
San Antonio, TX 78251

www.HomelessbyChoice.com

# Dedication

This book is dedicated to my family and the students I serve. To me, family isn't just the blood that runs through your veins but the love that is in your heart!

To my mom and stepdad, thank you for all your support through the years. I know it's hard for you to hear my stories. I don't share them to hurt you, but to inspire those going through life's storms. I love you both with all my heart.

To my dad, I hope one day we will be able to build a healthy relationship before it's too late.

To all my biological siblings, you have always been my motivation to never give up. We survived the storm and came out stronger. Our story is inspiring change all over the world. Thank you for allowing me to share it.

To my step-siblings, thank you for sharing your dad with us.

To my adopted parents, Pastor Doris and Pastor Johnny, thank you for loving me and caring for me when you didn't have to.

Finally, to the students, this book is for you. Never give up on life or your dreams. Life gets better, but you must put in the work. I hope this book inspires you. Remember, always better and never bitter!

# Contents

# Acknowledgments

I would like to acknowledge the following individuals who made this book possible.

Elizabeth Nerio, who started out as my intern and is now a trusted colleague. If it weren't for her, this book would not have been possible. She spent countless hours research and editing. Her professionalism, attention to detail, and creativity will help inspire thousands.

Michael Facciolo, my operations manager, made it possible for me to focus on the book as he took care of everything else. His support was crucial to me getting the book done.

Nathan Hassall, I am thankful I met this talented man. He taught me so much about writing, editing, and how to bring a manuscript to life.

Sheri Long and Ashley Yazarlou, thank you for being another set of eyes and volunteering to proofread the book. Your thoughts and comments helped me tell my story more accurately.

And finally, to all those who have helped me in the process of writing this book—and throughout life in general—that I have neglected to mention, I extend my thanks to you.

# Introduction

For the past eight years, I have attempted to write about my life. I have considered many ways to present my story, share my experiences, and introduce the individuals who have played a key role in my life. Each time I sat down with my laptop, I found myself in a new city, usually late at night in a diner. Even though diners can be busy in the evenings, I concentrate best in those circumstances. When I'm in need of a break from beating my brain, trying to resurface memories from my past, I'll stop, and people watch. If you enjoy people watching, there is no better place.

I find it challenging to resurface the memories of my childhood. I'm not sure if it's because my memories have thinned out as I've gotten older or if I've repressed them. It isn't until I encounter a particular sound or smell that brings them back to the surface of my mind. For example, a song on the radio that might have been playing during a traumatic moment in my life or the scent of a broadcaster's perfume that takes me back to a much better place in my youth.

I'm writing this book to share my life experiences and work with you in the hope that my stories inspire you. I promise that every story I tell will be told from the best of my recollection. I took the time to interview as many of the individuals in these stories as possible. Sadly, some are no longer with us, imprisoned or our encounter was too brief, and I do not know how to contact them. The individuals in my story that I have kept in contact with have helped me fill in the gaps of my childhood. This is my best effort to paint the most accurate account of my life.

My intentions are never to hurt anyone. For that reason, some of the names and locations in this book have been altered to protect those involved, but the stories have remained the same. The truth is, we are all human and are therefore flawed. The accounts of my life are filtered through my memory, beliefs, thoughts, and emotions. This makes them my truth. Each person in my journey has their own truth. I share this book with you with the best intentions in my heart.

I have traveled thousands of miles working in communities across the United States and abroad as a motivational speaker and activist fighting for homeless youth, families, and higher education. I stand in front of crowds, both large and small, sharing my personal story of growing up as a homeless teenager due to domestic violence. In the process, I've been asked by many, "Do you have a book reflecting your life story and work?"

I would give them the same answer: "I am currently working on my book."

My response wasn't a lie, I was working on it, but I couldn't get it done. I wanted to be able to sit down and write paragraph after paragraph of the great successes I've had in my life, but I couldn't. The issue may be because I still feel like I haven't accomplished enough, yet. There is so much more I am destined to do.

A dear friend and mentor, John Crowder, once said to me, "Roy, people want to hear your story. They want to learn from every aspect of your life. Don't worry about writing a bestseller or an insightful business book. Just write about your life and work."

So that's what I did. This book explores the highest peaks of my life; but more importantly, it also journeys through my lowest valleys. However, it was in those valleys that I learned some of my greatest life lessons! The lessons that taught me to forgive, to be better and never bitter, and to understand that we are all humanly flawed.

Some of the things in this book will probably surprise you. Some of you may not even like me after this, but this is my truth. One of the greatest lessons of being free is accepting who you are, flaws and all. Only then can we begin to shape and mold ourselves into who we want to be. I hope you enjoy some of the most significant moments in my life but also learn from my darkest moments.

# Foreword

It was to be another day, another talk where I got to share my story. But this audience was a particularly special group, comprised of federally employed women, a kindred experience for me as an Army Woman Veteran. This group, many of them veterans themselves, identified with my journey. Little did I know that a young homeless youth had snuck into my talk for the provided meal and—as we later learned—he ended up with food not only for his stomach, but also for his soul. Roy Juarez Jr. was not just hungry, but he was also searching for hope and peace from the chaos that life had dealt him.

Roy took my words, held onto them, and made a courageous move to change his life. As he puts it so eloquently, he chose to "Be Better, Not Bitter!"

The pages you are about to read will rivet you, anger you, make you laugh, smile, and maybe even move you to tears. Tomorrow does get better, and sometimes you have to give it several tries before you are confident that your circumstance will improve.

I have five daughters, and while I love them beyond words, Roy captured my heart and became the son I never had. Even though it was tough getting him to trust me and accept my mentorship, it was—and continues to be—a worthwhile experience. Roy tested me, challenged me, inspired me, and to this day makes my life a blessing. I must add, in the spirit of transparency, that I blame him for my premature grey hair. Now I have to color it more than I should!

Roy had been through countless amounts of pain and outright abuse.

Being too young to manage, cope, or much less forgive, he couldn't move on to explore his true gifts and potential. Like the peeling of an onion, each layer revealed his true gifts: Creativity, Innovation, Empathy, and Leadership. I recall an experience in 2005 when we served a fortune 500 company and many high-level executives thought Roy was already a college graduate with experience in business! The look on their faces when he disclosed that he was an intern and was still trying to finish college was priceless. Roy's work showed he had talent and a wittiness that—in spite of his lows—demonstrated he still loved life and was willing to use his experience to inspire change.

Read this book with the intent of filling your well, for unless you fill your heart with love, peace, and forgiveness like Roy did, you will live your life with an emotional scorecard always wanting to win, even if it means through manipulation or self-hate. Our story, as raw as it is, is about the true meaning of mentorship laced with the many tough lessons a homeless boy needed to learn in order to realize his true potential. We pushed and pulled, but ultimately, we held onto our powerful bond. Roy was me, and I was not going to allow him to end up just another statistic.

I am so proud of Roy and, frankly speaking, I was shocked that he asked me to write this foreword because I have probably been the toughest mentor in his life. I guess he knew that—in the end—love doesn't always mean kisses and hugs, but also truth, courage, and high expectations. Roy definitely is a much better person who has touched the hearts of thousands of youth and adults along his journey across the country and abroad.

I imagine every mentor hopes for the best for their mentee, I believe it is important to Live a Legacy rather than Leave a Legacy. Roy is one of my greatest Living Legacies. I see him on stage touching every generation with his love for humanity. Even though Roy has just started, I know that, in my heart, he will inspire many more individuals, for his purpose is still unfolding. He never ceases to amaze me.

Roy's story is the story of so many youth still living in the shadows. While not a celebrity that merely entertains for a moment, having Roy share his story can bring about healing, inspiration, provoke deep thinking about one's choices, and encourage anyone to keep going. Roy's story is a testament and an example that with the right decisions, mentorship, and forgiveness it will get better.

Love you Hijo and always remember I am here.

Consuelo AKA CCK
LTC (R) Consuelo Castillo Kickbusch
President and CEO
Educational Achievement Services, Inc.

*"Poverty is the worst form of violence."*

- Mohandas K. Gandhi

# CHAPTER ONE

## Meeting Morgan

"HOW CAN YOU love me? After everything I've done to you, how can you?" My mother cried in agony over the phone. She had found the rose and note I left on her windshield earlier that morning, before the sunrise.

"You're my mom! I love you! I will always love you."

That conversation always replays in my mind. At that point in our lives, we weren't very close. I loved my mother, but our relationship had been fractured by everything that had occurred in the previous years.

\*\*\*

### Dropping My Mom Off at the Airport

I never thought that our lives would turn out the way they have.

As I pulled into the Toledo Express Airport, I looked over to see my beautiful mother sitting in the passenger seat, smiling at me. Her jet-black hair sat just below her shoulders, and her olive skin was radiating from the sunlight. Although my mother is petite in stature, her spirit is that of a warrior. She was still standing after all that she had been through. The smile she wore spoke of her strength. It was the smile I had known as a little boy when times were good. The same smile I loved to run to as soon as I woke up, and the one that also put me to bed. I was happy to see her smiling again. We had made it through the storm, but we were left picking up the pieces of our lives.

Driving up to the curb, I thought, *She has no idea how much I love her.* Having my mother with me the past couple of days had been fantastic, and I didn't want to see her go.

"Mijo, thank you so much for bringing me out here. I can't tell you how proud I am of you," my mother said with tears forming in her eyes. "I love you so much… I want to give you something before I go." She rummaged through her purse.

"Mom, I love you too. And don't worry about it, you don't need to give me anything. I'm just glad you were able to come on such short notice."

She pulled out a handful of cash from her purse and handed it to me, "Here, it's money for a hotel."

"Thank you, Mom, bu-" I began to reply, but she interrupted me.

"Don't you dare tell me no, Roy! Take the money mijo, it's my gift to you."

I looked at the money for a second, and slowly moved my hand to accept the gift. I didn't want to fight with my mother over something sweet she was trying to do for me. Plus, staying in a hotel sounded nice! "Thank you, mom, I'll be sure to send you pictures of the hotel once I get settled in."

She sat there for a second before saying, "Okay mijo, this is it." She leaned in for a hug.

"Mom, I'm going to get out of the car to say bye! What kind of son do you think I am? I'm not Baby Ray," I laughed.

She laughed with me and replied, "Leave my baby alone!"

"Come on mom, he's not here! You can tell me. Who's your favorite son? Baby Ray or me?"

"Both of you are my favorite, but I will admit…"

I leaned over a bit, willing her to finally say it!

"You are my favorite oldest son!" She began laughing, but I wasn't amused.

I looked her dead in the eye and said, "Well then, you can get your own bags out of the trunk."

We laughed, and both got out of the car. I popped open the trunk to unload the carry on she had brought with her for the trip. As I tried to pass it to her, she looked down with her shoulders slumped. I took a breath.

"What's wrong, mom?" I asked as I put down her bag and gave her a hug.

"It's hard hearing you tell our story, mijo. Every time I hear you speak at an event I can feel the pain building up in my chest, and I can't help but cry. I feel terrible, but I know the kids need to hear it."

I hugged her tighter. It hurt me to see her in pain. I said, "Mom, we're not there anymore. We're in a much better place now and our story, our past, can help others."

"I know, you're right. You need to help the kids… it's just… hard," she wiped the tears from her eyes. "I'm so proud of you, mijo. I'll call you when I land."

I took a step back and placed my hands on her shoulders, looking into her glossy brown eyes. Trying to put a smile on her face I replied, "Naw, don't call me," which made her laugh.

"You're bad, Roy! Why did I ever have you?" She winked.

We hugged again.

"Fine. Call me when you get home safely," I said as I gave her a kiss on the forehead. "I love you mom, I'll see you soon okay? Have a safe flight and don't forget—I'm your best kid."

"I'll call you mijo, but I don't want you to drive so late at night. It's not safe." In her stern, motherly voice she continued, "You better use the money I gave you to get a hotel!"

"I will mom, I promise," I chuckled as I walked back to the driver's side of my car.

I watched my mother walk towards the automatic doors. Just before she went inside, she stopped and turned to give me one last smile. As she disappeared into a crowd of people, I thought about how amazing and strong my mother was. I am beyond blessed to be her son.

Driving out of the airport, my GPS was set for home. It was still early in the evening, so I figured I would be able to travel at least 4-5 hours that night. Eager to get back to my hometown, San Antonio, Texas, I thought about driving through the night. However, I promised my mother I wouldn't. I drove for about three hours, through the middle of nowhere. It was literally just acres and acres of farmland, but the lack of trees made for a beautiful sunset. I could see nightfall approaching. On the horizon, the sun was ready to rest for the evening, painting deep shades of reds and purples in the sky. As it said its final goodbye, the stars began to burn brighter against the darkness.

The lights of Indianapolis were shining off in the distance. I was near the outskirts of the city when I noticed a luminous yellow sign that read Waffle House. It caught my attention because the sign reminded me of the small tiles used in Scrabble—one of my favorite board games—and I was starving. I slowed down to examine the building. It seemed like a good spot, it wasn't my usual Denny's, but I thought, I'll give it a try. I pulled into the near-vacant parking lot and parked directly in front of the restaurant. Before I got out of my car, I reached over to the back seat to grab my new favorite book.

## The Waffle House

As I opened the front door of the diner, I was confronted with the sweet scent of waffles. I searched for a place to sit. The setup was typical of any American diner, a combination of booths and a long sit-down counter. What made this place stand out was the red leather upholstery that clothed the seats against the black metal framing. I was so tired that I decided to sit at the counter instead of waiting for a booth. I figured it would be entertaining to watch my meal be prepared. To be honest, I wasn't sure if I was supposed to wait to be seated or not, but I wasn't trying to find out. A middle-aged waitress, with 50s style reading glasses, approached me and asked if she could get me something to drink.

"Yes. Can I please have a glass of water, a cup of coffee, and an iced tea?" I asked.

She replied, "Of course, is someone joining you?" She pushed a menu in front of the empty seat next to me.

I smiled, "No Ma'am, I'm just really thirsty. I want the iced tea, but I need the coffee to wake me up and the water to hydrate."

"Well, okay… that's a lot of liquids, let me point you to the restroom now," she said laughing as she walked away.

Directly in front of me was my menu. As I read through it, everything sounded delicious, I really wanted a bacon cheeseburger with jalapeños and fries… but I couldn't be in a Waffle House and not get waffles!

When the waitress returned she set down my three drinks, chuckling to herself. "Alright thirsty man are you ready to order?" she asked.

"Well, I'm torn on what to order. I really want a burger and fries, but the pecan waffle sounds amazing!"

"Well, how hungry are you?" She said, willing me to make my decision.

For a second, I thought about getting both meals, but I had already gained 20 pounds on the tour. Finally, I said, "Okay, I either want the pecan waffles or a bacon cheeseburger and fries. As you can tell, I'm on a diet. You choose for me and don't tell me which one you chose, just bring it to me."

She asked, "Are you sure?"

"Yes, I'll love either one you bring me, I promise."

As she started to walk away, I called out, "Oh! If you choose the burger, can you add jalapeños?"

A puzzled look swarmed her face, "Jalapeños? You aren't from around here are you?"

"No ma'am, I'm from San Antonio, Texas. I'm just passing through," I smiled.

"Oh wow, you are a long way from home. Well, welcome to Pendleton," she said as she walked away.

"Excuse me. Did you just say you're from San Antonio?" An excited voice asked from a couple of seats down the bar. I turned and saw a pretty young lady who appeared to be in her early 20s, with shoulder length, light brown hair. She sat there smiling.

"You heard correct, I'm from San Antonio," I answered.

"That's crazy! I just came from visiting family there!"

"Oh, nice! What area were you in?"

The young girl looked confused, "Hm, I'm not really sure, to be honest."

"It's okay, San Antonio is a pretty big place. I was just asking because I grew up all over the city, so I would probably know where you were at."

She leaned over one of the empty seats, "I'm Morgan, by the way. What's that book you have? Is it Gandhi's autobiography?"

I looked down at my book on the counter. "Yeah, it's his book. Have you read it? Oh, and I'm Roy. It's great to meet you!"

"No, I haven't, but I love his work. I'll have to read it sometime."

"It's a great book! I think it really humanizes Mohandas Gandhi. You should definitely check it out," I smiled. "Did you know when he was younger, he used to beat his wife? And at one point he contemplated suicide?!"

Her head tilted to the side as she said, "Really? I never knew that."

"Neither did I until I read it. It just goes to show that you never know what a person has been through."

For a moment, I contemplated telling Morgan about my Homeless by Choice tour, but I didn't want to enter a long conversation. Most of the time I wouldn't mind, but I was desperate to read more of my book.

"So, what brings you up here?" she asked.

"Well, it's a long story, but basically I just finished speaking at a Youth Summit in Toledo, Ohio."

"Oh wow. What do you do?"

Usually, when I'm exhausted, and people ask what I do, I say I'm a banker. That's often the end of the conversation. In my mind, I was going to tell her I was a banker, but when I spoke, the words, "I'm a motivational speaker" came out of my mouth. I instantly regretted it and thought, *Great job Roy.*

"Really? That's very interesting. What do you speak about? Is there something in particular?" Morgan asked.

I knew she was going to ask that.

I quickly gave her my rehearsed elevator pitch, "I'm actually an advocate for at-risk youth and homeless teens. I travel the country trying to inspire students to stay in school, to not give up on life or their dreams and hope that—through my message—they can understand the value of higher education," I hoped it would answer all her questions and end the conversation.

I reached for my book to begin reading, hoping to give her a subtle hint, but her questions kept coming. "Wow. So what exactly is the message you give? I mean, how did you start speaking?"

I knew there was no way to get out of the conversation, which, deep down, I didn't really mind. I stopped trying to fight it. I finally gave Morgan my full attention when she asked,

"So Roy, What's your story?"

# CHAPTER TWO

## Fighting for my Future

IN MY MID-TWENTIES, I was a nontraditional college student. I had just completed my first semester at Hardin-Simmons University (HSU)—a private Baptist university—and I had spent the day packing up my dorm room which contained everything I owned. There I was, getting ready to move yet again. I was devastated about leaving, because this time, I really wanted to stay. I felt like a failure. The pain and fear from my teenage years resurfaced. I didn't have enough money to pay for the next semester at HSU. I had tried to figure out a way to raise the money but was unsuccessful. Time was ticking away, and I had 24 hours to figure out how to raise five thousand dollars to cover the difference in my tuition and lodging.

Defeated, I sat on the edge of my twin-sized dorm room bed. I could hear my friends in the hallway laughing and horsing around, as they were moving out of their rooms for the winter break. Usually, I would be right there joking around with them. I lived in an all men's dorm called Anderson Hall. On a typical day, you would find my dorm-room door open, so my friends could run in and tell me their latest jokes, talk me into doing something stupid, or tell me about their girl problems. Not this time though. My door was closed and locked. The last thing I wanted was for them to walk in and see the tears falling down my face.

My past was creeping back into my heart and mind. I felt the same anxiety I experienced when a family who had taken me in finally got the courage to tell me, "it's time for you to go." There were many times I wouldn't even wait for them to tell me. I became a pro at sensing when it was time for me to leave. Families would grow cold towards me, and there would be this detached look in their eyes. I just knew when they didn't want me. It was a horrible feeling, but what I hated most of all was the difficult conversation that came with it, and how uncomfortable it made them. So, I always tried to leave before they told me it was time for me to go because I didn't want to be a burden, and I understood I wasn't their kid or even really their responsibility. I am sure they each cared about me; but the truth is, I was an extra mouth to feed. So, I would thank them for the time I spent with them and would drag myself and belongings back to the street. Because of these experiences, each time I had to pack my bags, fear encompassed me. I never used to let anyone see it, because that's how people take advantage of you on the streets.

There I was, slumped over, staring at the blank space on the wall where my class schedule used to hang, reliving that horror all over again. I hadn't felt this type of fear for a long time. However, I understood that I had to leave. I didn't have any money for tuition, and I couldn't live there for free. I faced the question I had asked myself many times as a teenager, *Where do I go next?*

I looked at all the boxes I had packed, knowing that I had to lug them to my truck. I had reduced everything I owned to just 8 pale-brown boxes. That's a lot for me! When I was a homeless teenager, all my possessions fit into a single bag, which I called my home.

I had accepted defeat and thought, *Well, college was nice while it lasted, but being a college graduate isn't going to be a part of my story.* I lifted myself off my bed, so I could take the boxes to my truck when I noticed the crystal blue, octagon award I had neglected to pack sitting on top of one of the boxes. It was an award that had been given to my mentor by the Federally Employed Women's (FEW) organization, for speaking at their National Training Program, after her years of service in the United States Army. I pulled an old t-shirt out of one of the boxes, picked up the award, and dusted it off. As I admired it, my mind wandered off to when I had first found it.

\*\*\*

One day, let me rephrase that. One SCORCHING summer day in San Antonio, Texas, right before I left for college, I was cleaning my mentor's garage. Why? Because I was the best intern her company has ever had! She may tell you otherwise, but I know it's true, haha.

As I sorted through her boxes of business and personal items, I came across one that was full of accolades. Among them, a beautiful crystal-blue award caught my eye. I lifted it out of the box and read the inscription, *Federally Employed Women...* I realized this wasn't just any award. It was the award given to my mentor the night I first heard her speak. I was so excited, I stopped what I was doing and ran into the house.

My mentor, retired Lieutenant Colonel Consuelo Castillo Kickbusch, was sitting at her kitchen table checking her emails. As I approached, her slender eyebrows lifted to acknowledge my presence. I sat down opposite her and placed the award gently in the center of the table. The award was octagonal and had edges comprised of prisms. It was the perfect spot, as the sunlight poured in through the window and shone through the award, creating a kaleidoscope of color against the back of her laptop. Her rich, brown eyes peered over her screen, "Oh, you found my award. Thank you mijo."

I'm sure my mentor had no idea which award it was. She had boxes of them collecting dust in the garage.

I slowly began, "Mrs. K," which is how I lovingly refer to her, "Can I ask you something?"

She looked over at me, took off her glasses and placed them next to her laptop. "Of course, what's your question? Will I need the Tylenol?"

We both laughed. "No, not this time," I replied. "But what I wanted to say was, when you die, I don't want anything from you. Well, I take that back; there is one thing I want from you, but I don't want money or anything like that!" I quickly added.

She let out a chuckle and said, "Ay loco!" and with hesitation in her voice, she asked, "Okay, what is it that you want?"

"When you die, will you please leave me this award?"

She crinkled her eyebrows and picked it up. She asked, "Why this one?"

I pointed, "Look who gave it to you!"

She put her glasses back on and began to read the inscription out loud, "FEW steps into the future…" Revelation swept across her face. "This is the award I was given when you snuck in and heard me speak isn't it?" Her smile grew a little bigger.

I replied, "Yes ma'am, it is!"

She said, "Well if it's that important to you, it's yours. Take it with you back to college and put it somewhere where you can see it every day and know that if you don't graduate, I will hunt you down and kill you myself!"

We both laughed, I thanked her, put my sentimental gift away and reluctantly went back to finish cleaning her garage.

***

As I was standing in my dorm room holding the award in my hand, I was reminded of all I had lived through and how far I had come. I was so close that I couldn't give up now. After placing the award back on top of the box, I walked over to the sink and stared into the mirror as I wiped away my tears. In a faint voice, I told myself, "You got this Roy, you got this." I shook my head and raised my voice, "This is nothing compared to what you've been through. Think, Roy, think!" I repeated a mantra I used to say to myself when I was a homeless teenager, *No Excuses, Only Solutions*.

In the reflection of the mirror, I stared at my mentor's award sitting on the box, trying to figure out a solution. That's when it hit me. I began frantically opening box after box to find my iron and some nice clothes. After opening several boxes, I found them. I pulled out a clean button up shirt and a pair of pants. I gave them a quick press on top of my dorm room table and threw them on. Running out of Anderson Hall, I made my way past the HSU duck pond, towards the Johnson Building, where the Office of the President was located.

I am not exactly sure what I thought I would say or do, but I knew the president of the University was the highest person in charge, and if anyone could do anything, it was Dr. Turner. I was nervous and scared, but the idea of not receiving an education was more terrifying to me than having an awkward conversation with the president of my university.

As I approached the Johnson Building, my stomach started to turn, and I could feel my face getting warmer. Fear tried to persuade me to leave, but I knew I couldn't allow it to hold me back. I continued walking right through the front doors of the building; Dr. Turner's office was to the right of the entrance. Despite the doubt, I knew I had to try. I stood outside his office for a minute, inhaling deeply through my nose, trying to compose myself. The dull-brass doorknob reminded me of an eye. It taunted me. I mustered some courage, wiped the sweat off my palms on the back of my pants, reached forward, tightened my grip, twisted the doorknob, and entered the office.

As I walked in, I was greeted by his administrative assistant, who, with a beautiful smile said, "Hello, may I help you?"

With a nervous stutter in my voice, I said, "Yes, ma'am. I'd, um, I'd like to see President Turner, please."

She replied, "I'm sorry, Dr. Turner is very busy today, and he is not to be disturbed. Can I make an appointment for you, possibly next week?"

Her words hit me like a ton of bricks. *Next week?* I knew I didn't have until next week. I had to be out of my dorm room within the next 24 hours. I pleaded, "Is there any way to see him today?"

"No Sir, I'm sorry; you'll have to make an appointment."

At that moment I could feel my eyes swelling, heart racing, and the little hope I had left began to disappear. She must have noticed the change in my demeanor, the anguish that came over my face, because she then asked, "What is your name?"

"Roy Juarez, Jr.," I replied.

She gave me another warm smile and said, "Give me one second, Roy. Please wait right here."

She got up from her chair and disappeared into Dr. Turner's private office, shutting the door as she entered. My heart was pounding. I looked at the desk, everything was so orderly, not a single thing was out of place. Thoughts raced through my head. *What if this was it? What do I say if I get to see him? What if he doesn't have any time for me?* I stood there, sweat dripping from my brow, and silently prayed for help.

Dr. Turner's office door opened, and his assistant walked out. "You have two minutes, he will see you now."

I couldn't believe it. This was my chance, but what would I say? "Thank you, thank you so much," I uttered as I made my way past her desk and into Dr. Turner's office.

As I entered the room, Dr. Turner was sitting behind his desk surrounded by paperwork. He radiated a quiet confidence as he stood up and greeted me with a firm handshake. "You must be Roy. You need to speak with me?"

"Yes, sir."

I couldn't hold it in anymore. I started to weep and said, "Dr. Turner, this is my last chance. Please, I need to be educated. Sir. This is my last chance!"

Dr. Turner was surprised at my emotional outburst. With concern, he asked, "Roy, what's going on?"

In a voice of defeat and with my head hanging low, I said slowly, "Sir, you don't get it. I have fought so hard to get here, and I'm short on tuition. I've already packed up my dorm room in order to leave tomorrow, but sir, I can't go. I need to be educated. Don't you see? This is my *last* chance."

At this point, he got up from his seat, walked around and sat on the front edge of his desk, directly in front of me. I sat there, leaning back, with my eyes at my feet.

"Roy, how much money are you short?"

Briefly, I glanced up at him, but in embarrassment I bowed my head once more. I took a deep breath and said, "Sir I am short $5,000." I looked back at him for a reaction.

He stood there in silence and sighed deeply, staring at me. I feared what he was going to say next. I knew my future rested on his decision. Every second was an eternal tick. After flicking his eyes from side to side, he finally settled his gaze on me again. He exhaled, "Roy, go unpack your dorm room. I will find the $5,000 for you."

Tears filled my eyes. I couldn't believe it.

"Really sir? Really? You mean it?"

"Yes, Roy, now go unpack your dorm room. I will find you that money."

To say I was in shock is an understatement. I don't know what I really expected to happen when I decided to reach out to him. It was desperation. I

HAD to be educated. All my teachers who encouraged me to go to college told me time and time again that I needed to be educated because education would change my life. For the longest time, I lived my life trying not to be noticed; this was a lesson I had learned on the streets. Growing up as a homeless teenager, you learn to become invisible, it's part of survival. If you're invisible, people allow you to stay in their home longer, which means you have food to eat and a place to sleep. I had become so good at being invisible that I forgot I had a voice. That day, in Dr. Turner's office, I learned a huge lesson. Never be afraid to use your voice.

Usually, I was scared to ask for help because I didn't want to cause any trouble or inconvenience anyone. But this time, I was fighting for my future, my life. I realized that the worst that could happen was for Dr. Turner to turn me away. If he said no, my situation would have remained the same. There was no gamble, but there was something I could win. I'm glad I learned this lesson so early on during my college days because—unknowingly—it prepared me for the numerous times I would have to use my voice before graduating from college.

This gesture of mercy and compassion by Dr. Turner moved my heart so much that I wanted to give back to HSU in honor of him. I was sure I wasn't the only student going through something like this. During my few hours of spare time from classes, homework, or one of the three jobs I worked to support myself through college, I developed what I considered to be a win-win situation. I wanted to help other students like myself, students who might be at risk of dropping out due to the lack of emotional or financial support. With plenty of brainstorming, I developed a mentoring program called "Student 2 Student".

I put together a PowerPoint presentation about why it would be important for HSU to implement the program, making sure to highlight its student retention rate and financial benefits. I set up a meeting with Dr. Turner and the Dean of Students, Mr. Forrest McMillan, to present my ideas. They loved the concept and gave me the green light to start Student 2 Student immediately.

Dean McMillan and I reached out to faculty and staff to help us identify

8 mentors and 24 mentees. Each mentor was responsible for monitoring three mentees. Their primary objective was to help their mentee get connected to the resources provided by the university and the city of Abilene, Texas. As mentors, we had weekly meetings to evaluate the progress of our mentees and received ongoing leadership development training. The incredible part of the experience was being able to turn the Student 2 Student Program into a work-study position. This meant our mentors were paid for their time!

I genuinely believe it's important to be grateful to those who show us kindness. The concept of being grateful was a lesson I adopted as a homeless teenager. I knew people didn't *have* to help me, feed me, or care for me, so when they did, I was grateful. It hurt every time a family asked me to leave, but I always appreciated the time I had spent in their home. The kindness and generosity that Dr. Turner and Hardin-Simmons University had shown me made it easy to call HSU my home.

# CHAPTER THREE

## I Will Get the Money, I Promise

WHILE FOUR YEARS may seem like a long time, it really isn't. After countless pots of coffee and weekly cram sessions, I had finally made it. It was my senior year of college, and it had just been confirmed that I was going to graduate with my Bachelor of Business Administration from HSU, a day I thought would never come. Living as a homeless teenager made the dream of becoming a college graduate very difficult to envision, but still, I dreamed. Now it was finally happening!

I stood in line at the Grad Finale, a one-stop shop for all our graduation needs. The large conference room was set up with several booths. Each one helped us order something different. I wanted to get as much as I could, but my wallet wouldn't allow that. I settled with only ordering my cap, gown, and class ring. I was in shock; I kept telling myself, *You're going to have a degree!*

The night before, I had reached out to my mom and mentor to make sure they saved the date for my graduation on their calendar. Being a smaller school, graduation was held on campus in Behrens Chapel, and seating was limited. Every student was allocated the same number of tickets for their family and friends to attend.

I signed up for the essentials and, being at the end of the line, I was ready to receive my tickets. As I approached, the lady who was taking down the student ID numbers and distributing the graduation tickets looked up to see me grinning ear to ear. Her face warmed to mine as she asked politely, "May I please have your student ID?"

I handed it over to her and she ran my number. The anticipation was killing me, I was so excited. All those years of struggle, all that hard work. I was finally going to have something to show for it. I started to dream of what graduate life would be like, and how everything was falling into place. When I remembered where I was, I noticed that the lady had my ID for longer than I had anticipated. Still smiling, but a little confused, I asked her what was up. She clenched her teeth slightly and shook her head before leaning closer to the screen. Extending her arm slowly, the lady passed me my student ID back and said in a low tone, "I'm so sorry, Roy, but I can't give you any tickets."

A wave of confusion ran over me, "Why? What's wrong?"

"You have a balance on your account and, in order to receive tickets for graduation, you have to pay off the remaining balance."

My heart began to race as I said, "If I am unable to pay off my balance before graduation… will I… will I be able to graduate?"

She looked at me and let out a short, ironic laugh, replying, "Oh, of course, you'll still graduate!" I was so relieved to hear her words, but then she continued in a serious yet cautious tone, "It's just that none of your family can come to see you cross the stage."

My heart sank, *How could this be?* I've worked so hard to get to this point in my life. For a second I thought, *Why can't anything come easily? Why do I always have to fight?* I quickly reverted back to my life mantra and thought to myself, No Excuses; Only Solutions.

Still standing in front of the lady, I asked, "Is there anything I can do?"

"Well, if I were you, I would set up a meeting with the V.P. of Finance, Mr. Prescott. Talk with him and see what he can do."

I thanked her and left the room thinking about how to get past this new bump in the road. No Excuses; Only Solutions.

I went straight to the business office to set up a meeting with Mr. Prescott. Once I made it back to my dorm room, I started creating a plan because I didn't have the money to zero out my balance. During my four years at HSU, I had done so much to promote my university. I decided to compile a binder full of articles and documents of things I had done. I thought, *My contributions must hold some type of value.*

My binder was stuffed with every single thing I had ever contributed to the university. I was trying to build a strong case so that Mr. Prescott would allow my family to come to see me cross the stage. I inserted my Student 2 Student program, my volunteer work in the community, and also the program from the Donors Banquet where I shared my tempestuous story which helped raise thousands of dollars for the University. Everything was ready, and when the day finally came, I made my way to the business office. I sat outside the open door of Mr. Prescott's office, rehearsing what I was going to say, and how I would plead my case. My thought process was interrupted when he invited me in, "Come in here, Roy."

I walked in and looked at him, a heavyset man with pale skin, piercing blue eyes, and eyebrows that stood up like feathers.

"Good afternoon, sir." I extended my hand to shake his.

Instead of extending his hand towards me, he looked me up and down, then folded his arms across his chest. Leaning back in his chair, he demanded, "Where is my money?"

I was taken aback for a second because I didn't expect that reaction at all. It wasn't the type of behavior that reflected the spirit of HSU. Especially when our motto is to be a community dedicated to providing excellence in education enlightened by Christian faith and values. Nonetheless, he intimidated me.

Still standing, I said, "Sir, I will get the money, I promise."

He stared at me for a few seconds before responding, "I heard you are a motivational speaker or something?"

"Yes sir. I travel and share my story with students. I speak about growing up as a—"

He interrupted me, "Well, obviously you don't know how to manage yourself because if you did, you would have my money."

I was flabbergasted! Not knowing how to respond to his comment directly, I reverted to the speech I had rehearsed. "Sir, I have compiled a binder with all the things I have done for the university." I placed the binder on the desk in front of him and sat down to begin explaining the content, "If you open it up, you will see—"

He grabbed the binder and tossed it carelessly to the side of his desk. His words were sharp, "I don't care about the binder; I want my money."

Something shifted inside me. My pleading turned to rage. Mr. Prescott no longer intimidated me. He pissed me off. I came to this man for help. I didn't come with an attitude, I was calm and respectful. In return, he was rude, dismissive, and sought to silence my voice.

My inner street kid kicked in. Growing up on the street, I learned you had to stand up for yourself; that was Survival 101. As an educated person, I knew that didn't mean the situation had to get physical or disrespectful, even though part of me wanted it to! But, I knew I had a voice, and nobody was going to take that from me. In life, when people try to silence you, it is imperative not to give them that power. Your voice matters. You don't have to be rude or ugly when using it, but never let anyone take it away.

My tone deepened, and my body language went from, "Please let me share my situation" to, "You have no idea who you're talking to." It wasn't that I was a person with power or connections. However, I didn't survive the streets and fight so hard my entire life just to get to the point where some power-hungry snake could use his title to belittle me.

I sat up, leaned forward, stared at Mr. Prescott dead in the eye and said, "Let me tell you something." He jerked back in his chair. "I will be very successful one day, and you will be coming to me for money. Yes, I speak all over this country, and I tell my story about growing up as a homeless teenager. I talk about how great Hardin-Simmons is and how my university has always been there for me. So, you have a choice; I can tell the story about how my university was there for me all the way until the end or how at the very end they kept my family from seeing me cross the stage because of money. How do you want this story to be told?"

His eyes sharpened like daggers, as if I were his prey. He tapped his pen on the desk. His mouth twitched as he forced his body to relax. Reluctantly, he asked, "How many tickets do you want, Roy?"

I changed my voice back to my normal, calm tone, and said, "Sir, I don't want any more than the other students are getting. I just want my family to be able to see me cross the stage."

He snarled, "The tickets will be in your student mailbox this afternoon."

I thanked him and walked out of his office.

To this day, I am not sure why Mr. Prescott was so hostile towards me. Maybe he had heard something negative about me, or perhaps he just didn't like me; I will probably never know what his problem was. I had never crossed paths with him before this incident, and hopefully, I never have to again. I read online that he retired several years after our altercation, and thankfully so.

In life, we will never be able to please everyone, nor should we try to. Yes, it is important to work towards being a better person, but you don't have to lose your voice in the process. There is so much anger and hatred in this world; let us not add or fall victim to it.

While that wasn't the most positive interaction, it was not reflective of my overall experience at HSU. I absolutely love my alma mater; it is filled with amazing, gifted individuals who genuinely care about student success. I owe a great deal of gratitude towards many of my professors, including Dr. Patterson, Dr. McIntyre, Dean Worley, and Dr. O'Sullivan. Thank you for making my time at HSU amazing!

## The Call

Graduation was three months away, and I could barely contain myself. It was bitter-sweet. My friends and I had just spent four years together becoming like family, and in one night, our lives were going to change forever. While some of my friends had the next chapter in their life already planned out, I found it surprising that many of them didn't have a clue what they were going to do next. How could they not know? Maybe that was the street kid in me. Every time I moved into someone's house, all I could think about was my next step. Whose house would I go to next? For months leading up to graduation, I had been researching master's programs and applying for jobs on the East Coast. I had every intention of moving East and continuing my education; however, that all changed with one phone call.

I was in my dorm room getting ready to go to dinner when I heard my phone buzzing. It was my mentor calling, so I quickly picked up the phone, and halfway through my hello, she got straight to the point, as she always did.

"What are you doing for your country?" She barked like a drill sergeant. Being a retired lieutenant colonel, it's a fitting greeting for her.

I chuckled, "Well, I'm about to become a college graduate!"

"Good! It's about time!" she joked.

We both laughed.

"Well, how are you doing mijo? Are you excited?"

"I'm great, and yes, I'm ecstatic!" I replied. "Can you believe I'm going to graduate already? It feels like just yesterday your husband was driving me to HSU as a freshman! Will David and the girls be coming to graduation? Wait, you're coming, right?"

"Of course I'll be there, I wouldn't miss it for the world! But unfortunately, David can't make it because he's got to stay home with the twins. He still jokes that the majority of your boxes were shoes! I want to make sure you cross that stage. Which is actually why I'm calling you. What are your plans after you graduate?" she inquired.

"I plan to move to the East Coast and get into a master's program. I've been looking up schools in New York," I explained.

"I see," she said, followed by a short pause. "Well, I think you need to come work for me."

"Excuse me?"

"You need to work for me."

"Thank you for the offer Mrs. K, but can I at least think about it?"

"Of course mijo. You have from now until the end of this phone call to give me an answer."

It was difficult to be put on the spot like this, but this woman had become more than my mentor. She was like a second mother to me. I had grown to trust her, and I don't trust people easily—another side effect of being abandoned as a teen. Mrs. Kickbusch had helped me get to this point in life, and I felt she had my best interests at heart. So, without further hesitation, I said, "I would be honored to come work for you."

"Great! Welcome to Educational Achievement Services!" She said as she hung up abruptly, leaving me no chance to change my mind.

I was excited to finally be an employee of Educational Achievement Services (EAS). I had been an intern for many years, and the thought of having a job with my mentor was comforting. However, I must say, although Mrs. Kickbusch is brilliant, she is a very tough woman to work for. She has extremely high standards for her employees and even higher standards for me. Oftentimes I would think that I couldn't make her happy, but each time I reached her expectations, she would look at me, smile, and say, "I knew you could do it, Roy."

***

I recall one night working late on a project for a major corporation. I assembled all the documents we needed for our presentation to the CEO and his staff. Mrs. Kickbusch walked into the office and looked at me, surprised. "You're still here?" She asked.

I stood up and replied, "Yes ma'am, but I just finished the last packet."

"Ah, great mijo! Let me see what you've got."

With pride, I handed her the packets. She opened the first one, then the second one, and her eyebrows began to tighten, by the third one, she fanned the edge of all the packets. She sighed. I quickly ran through my mental checklist, *what had I forgotten?* I had printed everything we needed, put all the pages in order, and stapled them together. I made sure to do quality control by double checking each kit so that I didn't miss anything. She tossed the packets onto my desk.

I asked, "Is everything okay? I doubled checked everything."

She snapped, "What is this?" as she gestured toward the packets on the table.

I was confused. "Did I miss something, ma'am? I double checked them all," I repeated.

She picked up the packet that was on top of the stack and extended her arm to give me a better look. "The staples are at a diagonal; they need to be parallel with the top of the paper. Do you expect me to give these to the executives?" I sat there, confused, before she ordered, "Do them all again."

*WHAT*?! My face quickly turned to see if she was serious. All of them? All over? It was already 9:00 p.m., and I had been working all day. That meant I was going to be working way past midnight. I couldn't understand why she was so mad that my staples were diagonal and not parallel with the top of the paper. *Who cares?*

I'm sure she noticed how confused I was. She interrupted my thoughts with, "Roy, sit down. Let me tell you a story."

I reluctantly sat down because the last thing I wanted to do was hear a story. I didn't have time for a story, I had packets to prepare. She explained:

"I am a daughter of a maid. As a young girl, I didn't think much of it. I knew my mami (mother) worked very hard; but it wasn't until I was a little older, that I learned the lesson I am about to share with you."

Despite my fatigue, I wanted to give my mentor as much respect as possible, so I sat up straight and gave her my undivided attention.

She continued, "After school, I would rush to the hotel to help my mom clean rooms. This would help her finish her work sooner, and she was then able to get home to prepare supper for my siblings and me. As a typical kid, I did not want to clean hotel rooms. My mother would say, 'Consuelo ven pa ca.' (Consuelo come here).

I would reply, '¿Si mami?' (Yes mom?)

'Take this brush and go clean the other toilet.'"

She scrunched her nose as though replaying the moment in her mind.

"I would reluctantly grab the brush and start to walk towards the other toilet. My mother would then call out, 'But Consuelo, don't just scrub the toilet, make it sparkle.'"

My left eyebrow lifted, I did not understand what her mother meant by sparkle.

Mrs. K took a deep breath, "I would grumble and complain as I walked away. One day my mother heard me talking back under my breath and said, 'Consuelo! What did you say?'"

I could see my mentor reliving the moment. She paused before her lips lengthened into a grin. "To keep from getting in trouble, I told her I had said: 'I love you.' However, one time I got brave enough to ask her, 'Why do I need to make the toilet sparkle? It's just a toilet.'"

Her grin disappeared, and the tone of her voice changed, I couldn't tell if it went soft or was sprinkled with pain.

She continued, "It was at that moment my mother taught me a valuable lesson, and tonight, I pass it on to you. That day, I saw something in my mom that I had not seen before. There was a hint of sadness in her eyes. She said to me, 'Consuelo, to you, I may only be a maid. To the world, I may only be a maid. But let me tell you something, I am not just any maid. I am a world class maid. Every morning when we line up, the boss calls my name, 'Castillo, good job! Your rooms have received compliments.' See Consuelo... don't just do a job, but do a job so well done that even when you aren't there, your work speaks for you.'"

Mrs. K's eyes glossed over, "Mijo, I am not making you do these kits all over again because I want to be mean. I want to teach you about the quality of your work, the same lesson my mother taught me. Do a job so well that even when you aren't there, your work speaks for you."

She paused for a moment, looking up at the ceiling, before she resumed in a softer tone, "I know I can be tough on you, but it's because I believe in you, Roy. I want you to be extremely successful. Now hurry up and redo these kits! We have a meeting to get ready for!"

What I didn't realize at the time was my mentor was giving me something priceless—her wisdom. The story she told me that evening set the bar for my level of professionalism and quality of work.

***

Graduation was three months away, and I had a job secured! I guess I wasn't headed for New York but living in Vegas didn't sound too bad. Working for my mentor was going to be tough, but I was excited to be part of the team, and I was ready for the challenge.

# CHAPTER FOUR

## A Hunger to Leave the Streets

F INALLY, GRADUATION DAY had arrived. In some ways, it still felt surreal. I had always wanted to graduate from college, but never thought it would be my reality, especially as a homeless teenager. It wasn't until I was getting dressed for the ceremony that it really began to set in. I remember thinking, *Man, how did I get so lucky?*

I knew the odds were stacked up against me from the start, but somehow, I was able to navigate myself from the streets to a university. It was bittersweet because I kept thinking about all the other kids who grew up like me; did they get this lucky too? I didn't think about that for too long, because I didn't want to get myself down. I wanted to enjoy the moment I fought so hard for.

I was excited because my sisters, mom, mentor, grandma, great-grandmother, and a handful of other people who I hold dear to my heart were coming to the ceremony. I may have had to fight a little harder to get their tickets so they could watch me graduate, but it was worth it just to have them there.

What made this occasion even more special was the fact that everyone I had invited was traveling so far to share this moment with me. My family drove four hours North, my mentor and one of my best friends—Goy—flew in from out of state. If these weren't reasons enough to be overjoyed, I had yet another reason. It was important to me that my great-grandmother would be able to see me graduate. She was approaching her 90th birthday and wasn't in the best of health, so knowing that she would be there was a dream come true. All this excitement made the hours building up to graduation drag on. However, I knew that once I crossed the stage, no one could ever take my degree away from me. That's the power of education.

All the graduates were standing outside of Behrens Chapel, waiting to make our grand entrance. As I moved closer to the door, I could hear the music playing inside the building. I was beyond excited and in disbelief. Right before I walked into the Chapel, I heard someone yell, "Roy!" I turned to where the sound came from. It was my friend, Tyler, who gave me a huge smile and a thumbs up.

I smiled back and walked into the Chapel.

I was anxious but tried not to get too ahead of myself. I wanted to enjoy every moment. For many people, higher education is a natural progression after high school. For others, it's a choice. For me, it was a dream I thought I'd never get the chance to fulfill. I had accepted the lie that I didn't get to have dreams because I was homeless and came from a broken family. Standing there in my cap and gown, I realized my dream was just minutes away.

As we walked down the aisle, I felt excitement fill the air. Family members were waving at their soon-to-be-graduates, some holding a bouquet of roses, and others with balloons that read, *Congrats Grad!* That's when I finally spotted my family in the audience, and it all fell into place. Everything was in slow motion. I could see my mom clapping, my grandma waving, and then I noticed my great-grandmother. It was at that moment that I remembered why I fought so hard.

When it comes to education, I know its value is far greater than a piece of paper with a name written on it. For me, education is freedom. Freedom from the streets, freedom from poverty, and freedom for *mi familia.*

As I sat through the ceremony, I was filled with contrasting emotions. I was excited to be graduating, but also sad that this chapter in my life was ending. I would be leaving friends who had become like family. People like Lorrie Whitlock and Santos Montoya who were my roommates, senior year. To be honest, Lorrie had graduated a year before us and supported us on an "I owe you." She paid for everything, rent, food, utilities as we worked to finishing college. I eventually paid her back, but I am not sure if Santos did. He married her, so I guess his debt is paid off. Haha. Then, there were people like Amy Lane, my boss at First Financial Bank; Yolanda Alamilla, a coworker who became a close friend; or Celestina "Blue" Garcia, whose family had allowed me and my best friend, James Alvarez, to crash their family gatherings. I'd be leaving my boys; Jonathan Sharrett, Jesse Ontiveros, Matt Harmon, Shawn Clemons, and Sandy "Fig" Figueroa. These are just a few of the many people who would keep me going when I was missing home or when I felt like I couldn't make it anymore. Our lives were about to change for the better, but God I knew I would miss them... and I still do.

Finally, it was time. The row in front of me stood up to make their way to the stage, which meant my row was next. My nerves started to kick in. My heart was beating so hard that—if people in the audience weren't cheering—everyone would have heard it! My palms were sweaty, but I was grinning ear to ear. I was anxious. But it wasn't because I was crossing the stage or shaking the newly appointed President Hall's hand, it was because of everything I had been through up to this point. I had finally made it. I was just about to officially graduate!

The usher signaled for my row to stand up. We headed towards the stage. You could see the excitement in everyone's faces. I watched as each person ahead of me received their diploma until finally, just one person was standing between my dream and me. When they called my name—and I was finally able to walk across the stage—everything I had overcome was rushing through my mind. The time I had to work under the table digging ditches for extra money, when I had to survive off ketchup packs because I had nothing else to eat or when I slept in the back of someone's car because their kid didn't want me in their house. It may have been a short walk, but the journey to get there had been long and arduous. In those few steps walking across the stage, I had proven to myself and others that it doesn't matter where you start in life. With hard work, perseverance, and a desire for a better future, anything truly is possible.

My past did not define who I was. Although I couldn't see my family from the stage, knowing that they were there to witness this pivotal moment in my life was remarkable.

After the ceremony, I walked outside the auditorium to find my family. When I finally found them, they crowded me with hugs. I had become the first in my family to graduate from college. Standing there with a little gift in her hands was my fragile great-grandmother. Her timeworn face didn't affect her beauty, and her brown aged eyes brightened as she smiled at me. Seeing how proud my family was of me made all my hard work and sacrifices worth it. We all talked and joked for a bit. My sister Tammy was scrolling through the ceremonial program, searching for my name, as she said, "Shoot, if even you can graduate from college, then I know I can graduate from college!"

We stood there laughing and taking pictures for a while. I think my grandma thought it was her graduation because every professor I introduced her to, she wanted a picture with them. I love my grandma; she's so crazy.

At HSU, there is a circular wall that lists the names of everyone who has graduated, and they had just added my name. I thought it would be the perfect place to take more pictures! My family and I traced our fingers on the wall, searching for my name. Truth be told, I just wanted to know if it was actually there. Although I'm somewhat joking, I do check my alma mater every time I visit just to make sure that they haven't removed it!

Once we had finished taking what felt like hundreds of pictures, my mentor, Dr. Bridges—who came to see me graduate—walked up to us and surprised me by saying he had made us all dinner reservations. Dr. Bridges and his wife, Charlotte, are an extraordinary couple. When Dr. Bridges was a young professor, he began mentoring Mrs. Kickbusch when she was a student at HSU. When I moved to Abilene, he became my mentor as well.

I got in the rental car with Goy, who flew in with my mentor, and we headed to the restaurant. It was great to have him there. Goy and I had gone to Southwest High School together, he was actually my first friend and one of the only ones I've kept in contact with. It was strange to have a friend named Goy because my name is Roy, and people always teased us about it.

Goy had grown to be more like a brother, my sister Amy would lovingly refer to him as her "chocolate bunny," and I have no clue why. I laughed as I wrote this… I get the chocolate part because he is darker skinned, but where she gets the bunny from, I'm dumbfounded. He doesn't have big ears. It must be one of their inside jokes. I would understand if she said a cuddly bear because of his size, but nope, he's a bunny. As he drove, I gazed out the window, and my mind went back to the thoughts I had earlier that day while getting dressed. *How did I actually become a college graduate? How did I get so lucky?*

***

In 1997, I was on the streets of downtown Dallas, Texas. I remember searching for my next meal, my next place to sleep. Then I saw it, an enormous, beautiful hotel. *They have to have food in there*, I thought. So I made my way in and started scanning the lobby. I walked towards the conference area, seeing what I could find. I came upon a long line of women waiting outside a conference hall.

I didn't want to bring attention to myself, so I pretended to be unphased and walked right past them. I searched for a place to hide my bag because I knew one way or another, I was going to get into that room. I found a safe place between a couch and a fake tree. As I walked towards the line of women, the conference doors opened, and they started to file in. I jumped in line with them, hoping to blend in enough. I was extremely nervous that someone might stop me, but to my surprise, nobody did; I made it in!

I couldn't help but notice how beautiful it was. The room was full of round tables dressed in crisp white tablecloths and set with wine glasses and fancy cutlery. I stared at the set up for a minute and took it all in. I knew it was just a conference room, but to me, it was the most beautiful place I had been in a while. My attire didn't match the occasion, and if I didn't find a seat quickly, I was sure they'd ask me to leave. I made my way to the furthest table towards the back corner of the room and took a seat.

While I was sitting there, ladies began taking the empty seats next to me. I received a few concerned looks, but no one said a word. In an effort to blend in, I began asking questions about where they were from or if they were enjoying the conference. Most of them went along with the conversation, which made me feel a little less out of place.

The conference had started, and I couldn't care less. I was only there for a meal, and a Caesar salad and dessert were already on the table waiting for me. Not wanting to bring any more attention to myself, I waited until everyone else was seated and started eating their salad before I began to devour mine.

The salad was delicious, but I really didn't get a chance to enjoy it because I ate it so quickly. I was left with an empty plate sitting in front of me while everyone else continued to enjoy theirs. Before I knew it, the server had taken my empty salad plate away and replaced it with the main course, it was baked chicken breast, wild rice, and diced potatoes. I started scarfing down the food when the lady next to me passed me the bread basket. I placed one on my plate and took a few extra for later. To best describe the scene, I felt like Jack Dawson from the movie *Titanic* when he was eating with all those rich people.

I thought to myself, *Roy don't eat this too quickly.* I was enjoying my chicken, but my eyes were fixated on the luscious chocolate cake topped with whipped cream, sitting in the center of the table. I couldn't wait to eat it. At that moment, a woman came onto the stage. Honestly, I wasn't interested in what she had to say because I was almost done with my meal and was about to move on to dessert. But her words caught my attention, she spoke with an authority that mesmerized the entire audience. When she began talking about her life and the way she was raised, I completely forgot about the cake sitting in front of me.

She shared her story about growing up on the third to last street in Laredo, Texas. As a daughter of immigrants, she was faced with many challenges like poverty, illiteracy, and discrimination.

When she was in high school, her guidance counselor told her that girls like her didn't make anything of their lives, they just made babies. Distraught, she sought comfort in her father. He taught her to use her voice.

He told her, "Did you ask her, why not you? Go back to that counselor, and you ask her why you can't have your dreams." Her father reminded her that just because they were poor, that didn't give her permission to think poorly or behave poorly. He also told her, "You are not poor! You are rich! Rich in culture, rich in values, rich in familia, but most of all, you are rich in faith, in a God who can make anything happen. Don't you ever tell me you are poor or that you can't do something. There isn't anyone that's poor in this house."

With a mentality like that, this lady grew to be the highest-ranking Latina woman in the combat support field of the United States Army and broke all kinds of records. All because she learned to value her worth, the worth of others, and always asked, "Why not me?"

These were more than just words to the homeless kid who had snuck in. I sat there repeating to myself the same questions her father taught her, *Why not me? Why can't I have my dreams?* I started to remember all the dreams I had growing up, dreams I had not thought of in a long time. Dreams of becoming an astronaut, geologist, lawyer, actor or storm chaser, and even being a high school graduate. The problem was, I had accepted my current situation as an absolute. I thought, *This is the best my life is going to get. I have to find a job, work it really hard, and make the best of it.*

That day, something inside of me changed. I realized that it was up to me to decide who I will be and where I will go. I am the author of my life, and that means I get to write the ending. The speaker's words kept playing in my mind like an old record, *Why not me? Why can't I have my dreams?* There were so many reasons why society could have given up on me; the fact that I was homeless, came from a broken home or because I was a high school dropout. The truth is, I couldn't have my dreams because I had given up on myself. What I've come to learn is this, the gift of dreaming is a gift we give ourselves, and no one can take our dreams from us. We can choose either to keep our dreams or give them away.

We give our dreams away little by little, each time we buy into the idea that we aren't smart enough, attractive enough, tall enough, fast enough or educated enough. Buying into those ideas kills the dreams inside of us. I learned never to give my dreams away to anyone or give into my situation. I always ask myself, *Why not me?*

The speaker lit a fire in me. I sat there on the edge of my seat, mentally devouring her every word. I walked into that room hungry, but now there was an even bigger hunger inside of me. A hunger to leave the streets, reunite my siblings, and chase my dreams.

I was so lost and broken, but that night I was feeling something I had not felt in such a long time; I was feeling hope. I sat there in awe, and when the woman finished speaking, the entire room stood up and gave her a huge ovation. I knew that was the perfect moment for me to make my exit and not get caught, but there was no way I was leaving. I needed to meet this lady, so I risked it and stayed. As soon as the event ended, I rushed towards the front of the room where I saw the woman had sat down. As I got closer, I realized there was a long line of people who also wanted to meet her. At this point, I didn't care who saw me. When it was finally my turn, I didn't even know what to say; I merely took her business card and thanked her.

As I walked away, I knew my situation was the same, but I wasn't. Even though I was motivated, I was still filled with self-doubt. I said to myself, *Roy, do you really think you can do it?* But I battled the negative thoughts with, *Well, even if I don't make it, I am going to make sure that my little sister and baby brother do. They will have their dreams.* I walked out of the conference hall and grabbed my bag.

I made my way back to San Antonio and went straight to Mrs. Carmen's house. Mrs. Carmen—one of my close friend's aunt—had agreed to care for Baby Ray when we became homeless. I didn't know what I was going to do, but I knew I was going to get my baby brother back. He was going to have the opportunities I never did, even if that meant sacrificing my dreams.

When I got to Mrs. Carmen's house, I explained to her I had found a place for my brother and me to live, even though it wasn't the truth. I thanked her for all she had done for him, then took Baby Ray with me to a church we used to attend. There was always something going on, so I figured someone had to be there. When we arrived, the church was locked up and the parking lot was empty. As Baby Ray and I were hanging around outside, I saw a white van pull in. I saw a female silhouette in the driver's seat, but I didn't realize it was the senior pastor, Doris Zorola, until she got out of the van.

She saw me and said, "Roy, it's been so long! How are you doing?" in her soft Southern accent.

Pastor Doris looked exactly how I remembered her. The same beautiful dirty blonde hair with huge curls. She was always so well put together.

I replied, "I'm fine, Pastor Doris. Can I talk to you?"

"Of course. Come on; let me open up the church." She proceeded, "How's school?"

"I dropped out."

She stared at me in disbelief as we walked into the church.

Pastor Doris made her way into the sanctuary to turn on the lights. Baby Ray and I stood in the foyer underneath the giant cross that hung above us.

After a while, I decided to walk Baby Ray into the fellowship hall and sat him down at the first table nearest the door. I went back through the foyer and into the sanctuary. I stood at the back of the room so I could keep an eye on Baby Ray. Pastor Doris walked to where I was standing and asked, "So, what's going on, mijo? Is everything okay?"

I wasn't sure how to ask her, but I knew that I needed to find a place for us to stay. I was extremely nervous and scared. I swallowed the lump in my throat and started talking, "Pastor Doris, my brother and I don't have anywhere to live but..." I could see that she re-positioned her body to really listen to what I was about to say. I continued, "If you let us live here, in your church, I promise you... we will clean it, and it will be ready for all your services, every Sunday and Wednesday."

She stared at me in silence. I attempted one more plea with a desperate whisper, "We just need a place to live."

I stood there for a few seconds before she spoke, but it felt like forever. She said, "You're not gonna live here in this church..."

Hearing her say these words made my heart sink. I had no idea what I was going to do. Did I make a mistake by taking my brother from Mrs. Carmen's house? Where were we going to go? How would I care for him? I didn't have a Plan B. Actually, I didn't even have a Plan A. I just wanted a better life for my brother, but now I had made things worse; he would be homeless with me on the streets.

I began to turn to Baby Ray, to explain to him that we had to leave and go find somewhere else. As I went to speak, Pastor Doris continued, "You'll live with me instead... under one condition."

I froze, not sure if I had heard her correctly. *Did she just say we could live with her?* But those words—*one condition*—rang sharply in my ears. I had heard those words from every person who had ever taken me in, and the truth is, those conditions weren't always good. I could feel my walls going up to protect me from getting hurt again. With all the courage I could muster, I questioned harshly, "Well, what do you want from me?"

Taken back, she replied, "Excuse me?"

This time, with a little more anger in my voice, I repeated, "What do you want from me? Everyone wants something. What d'you want?"

Luckily, Pastor Doris saw beyond my explosive response and could see the broken kid inside me. In a compassionate voice, she said, "Roy. Roy, calm down." She walked closer to me and gently placed her hands on my shoulders. As I looked up at her, she continued, "All Pastor Johnny and I want is for you to go back to high school."

I believed her, but I didn't want to. Trusting her meant I had to lower my walls, and that would allow them to hurt me. I had dropped out of school because I never knew where I was going to live or how long I would last in any place. I asked, "That's all you want from me? To go back to school?"

She continued, "If you're gonna live in our home, you have to go to school."

Although I had my guard up, a small part of me felt relieved. That's all I really wanted, to be in school again. I was tired of living out of my backpack and not knowing where I was going to sleep at night, who was going to take me in, or what they going to want from me. I just wanted to be *normal* again.

Pastor Doris said, "I'll need to speak with your mom because she needs to know you're with me and I need her permission to take you in."

I nodded to let her know I understood.

That evening, Baby Ray and I went home with Pastor Doris. As we pulled up to her house, I knew the situation wasn't certain just yet. She hadn't even talked with her husband, Pastor Johnny, about us moving in. What if he said no?

Pastor Doris and Pastor Johnny live in a beautiful home in Atascosa County, out in the middle of nowhere. Their house sits on seven acres of land. As we drove down the long, familiar country road, I sat in silence, still unsure what my future would hold. Finally, I saw their house in the distance, obscured by trees in the middle of the lot. As we pulled in, she said, "We're home."

I thought, Sure we are. Let's see how long this one lasts.

I took Pastor Doris up on her kind offer and enrolled at Southwest High School. I was 17 years old and a third-year freshman when I started school for the last time. Southwest quickly became the best high school I attended. I'm not sure if it was the environment of the school, the fact that I had a stable home, or a mixture of the two, but I loved my time there. Before I knew it, I only had three more months until I would reach the most significant day of my life thus far, high school graduation. Honestly, I was scared because I didn't know what I would do next. Southwest had given me a second chance at being a normal teenager. I had made a ton of friends and was really involved with our after-school Bible study club, which we called, S.O.S. We met every Thursday in room 25, Mrs. Barrera's Spanish classroom.

Mrs. B was the sponsor of our bible study, and quickly became my favorite teacher! One Thursday, as soon as school let out, I made my way quickly to Mrs. B's room. I rushed through the halls because I wanted to get to her room early enough to speak with her privately.

As I helped her rearrange the room for our S.O.S. meeting, I said, "Mrs. B, I have a thought."

"Okay let's hear it."

I took a deep breath, then proudly shared my idea. "I think I should fail my English class, so I can stay here one more year and help you with S.O.S."

She stopped what she was doing and stared at me, trying to figure out if I was joking around or being serious.

She finally said, "Roy, you can't do that!"

"Why not ma'am? I've been in high school for five years already, what's one more year?"

"Roy, you can't fail on purpose. You must graduate and go to college."

"Mrs. B, what if I don't make it?" I asked.

Realizing how nervous I was to graduate, she tried to reassure me, "Roy, you are the strongest young man I know. You are going to make it. Promise me you will graduate."

"Alright, I promise."

Graduation was fast approaching, and life was about to throw me a curve ball. Of all the high schools I could have attended in San Antonio, I ended up attending the same school as my mom's boyfriend's son, Carlos. We were both seniors and graduating the same night.

A few weeks before my graduation, I called my mom to remind her about the big day. "Hey, mom! It's me, Roy," I said as she picked up the phone.

"Hi, mijo. How are you?" she asked.

"Oh, I'm fine Mom. I was just calling because I wanted to tell you something. I want to tell you... I made it! Can you believe it? I'm actually gonna graduate," my voice was shaking with excitement and disbelief.

She responded, "I knew it! I'm so proud of you. After everything we've been through, you're gonna make it."

She was right, we had gone through so much! "Well, thank you, Mom. I just wanna tell you one more thing."

"What is it?"

"I know that Carlos and I are going to graduate together, but I just wanna say, when we graduate, you're my mom."

She nearly cut me off when she asked, "Excuse me? What did you say?"

I was hesitant to repeat myself because of the tone in her voice, but I did anyway, "Well, mom, I'm just saying that when we graduate, you're MY mom."

She was so upset, she hung up on me without a word.

I placed the phone back on the receiver and stared at it for a while, thinking maybe, just maybe, she'll call back. But she didn't.

When graduation finally arrived, the people who I call my adoptive parents, the pastors who took me in, helped me get ready for graduation. Earlier in the week, Pastor Doris had taken me shopping for an outfit. On the day of graduation, I put on the new clothes she bought for me. I pulled up my black pants, buttoned up my white dress shirt, tightened my solid green tie, and slipped on the black shoes I had shined myself. I looked in the mirror like, "Damn! Who's that Papi Chulo?" I was ready to cross the stage.

Backstage, we were all excited. Everyone was taking pictures. Some of the girls were crying and making promises to never lose touch. Others were talking about the different parties that were happening that evening. I was standing by myself, trying not to cry. Once the ceremony started, they had us all lineup. One by one we walked through the opening in the curtain to receive our diplomas. As I waited my turn, I was trying to peek out and scan the audience. I was hoping to find my family, but it was too difficult, like a real-life game of Where's Waldo. There were so many people out there. Before I knew it the only person in front of me was my friend, Emery Johnson. The vice principal called his name, and he disappeared past the curtain. I was next.

As I stepped into the opening of the curtain, I could see everyone. I glanced at the entire colosseum, the crowd was enormous. As I stepped out of the opening, each step became history in the making for a kid like me. I had beaten the statistics.

My name was announced, and I walked forward. I was too anxious to receive my diploma, it was a proud moment for me because it was a milestone I thought I'd never reach.

Once the ceremony was over, I walked outside the Colosseum to find the people who came to support me. To my surprise, several families and individuals who had helped me out along the way had shown up. Even though I was glad they all decided to celebrate with me, there was one person I really wanted to see.

In between hugs and pictures, I was scanning the crowd looking for my mom. Finally, I saw her. As I began walking toward her, our eyes met. She stepped towards me. As we got closer, I noticed she was crying. I said, "Mom! Mom, stop crying. We're going to be happy tonight. Pastor Johnny made reservations for us at Mi Tierra, the restaurant downtown."

I motioned for her to follow me as I started walking back to the group of people who had come see me. After a couple of steps, I realized my mom wasn't following me. I turned back, and she was just standing there in between myself and the people she came with. "Wait a minute guys! Hold on!" I shouted to my group of supporters. I turned back around and walked towards my mom again.

"Mom? Mom, what are you doing? They're all ready to go," I explained.

She stood there with her head down, unphased by what I had said. It was then I knew something wasn't right. "Well, Roy... it's just that, Carlos, he doesn't want to eat at Mi Tierra. We already have reservations somewhere else."

I looked at her the same way I always did when she let me down, and said, "Okay, so what are you telling me then, mom?"

"Well, mijo, what do you want me to do?" she replied.

I couldn't hold in my anger anymore, "Mom, you know what? Just say it. SAY IT, MOM! I just want to hear you say it! What are you telling me?"

In a broken voice she said, "Mijo, you don't underst—"

***

"Well, are you gonna stay in the car the whole time or are you gonna get out to eat?" Goy joked as I saw the backs of Dr. Bridges and his wife, Charlotte, disappear into Abuelo's. I still couldn't believe that I had just graduated from HSU.

It was like my thoughts had paralyzed me. I knew we were in the restaurant parking lot, but I couldn't seem to get my body to move. "Yeah man!" I laughed, "I'm getting out right now!"

I forced myself to snap out of my trance and got out of the car. I watched the car my mom rode in park a few spots down from us. She may not have been there for my high school graduation, but she made sure to be there for me this time around.

We all walked in and joined Dr. Bridges and Charlotte who were already sitting at our reserved table. Since it was a dinner honoring my accomplishments, I sat down at the head of the table. I noticed my mom appeared distant and almost confused like she didn't know where she should sit. I watched as she walked down to the very end of the table and sat on the left corner. Why would my mom sit in the furthest spot away from me? The rest of the table started to fill in. Mrs. Kickbusch and Goy sat to my left, and Dr. Bridges and Charlotte sat to my right. There was a look on my mom's face that I couldn't quite figure out. Then I realized it was a blend of shame and regret. I knew instantly that she was carrying the guilt of abandoning me in the past. She probably felt that she didn't deserve to sit next to me on my special day. I wasn't going to let my mother continue to carry that burden of guilt and shame in her heart. She had been through enough.

I turned to Mrs. Kickbusch and asked, "Ma'am, do you mind moving down a seat, so my mother can come to sit next to me?"

She looked at me a little embarrassed. "Oh! Of course, mijo! Your mother should be right here with you," she said as she moved down a chair.

"Hey, mom! What are you doing way down there? Your seat is next to me," I called across the table, pointing to the open chair.

I'm not sure if anyone else noticed my mother's demeanor that night but seeing her tormented by our past hurt me. I never wanted to add to the pain and brokenness my mother had experienced in her life. I knew she never intentionally tried to hurt me as a teenager; she was just broken and in an unfortunate situation. She loved me the best that she could, and I thank her for that.

My mom reluctantly stood up and slowly walked over to me. When she finally sat down by my side, something changed. She smiled at me, placed her hand on top of mine and said, "Thank you, mijo."

I smiled back.

I wanted my mom to know that despite our past, she was still my mom. Nothing was ever going to interfere with the love I had for her. My mom's place at the table was next to me, and it always will be. Seeing the smile she wore the rest of the night made dinner that much better.

## Back at the Waffle House

"Were your adoptive parents at your graduation? Are you still close to them?" Morgan asked.

"Yeah, I'm still very close to them, we talk as often as we can, but they were only at my high school graduation," I smiled.

The waitress walked over to me, "Hey thirsty man, your food will be right out. Do you want any more coffee or water?"

"Yes please, I'll take more of both."

Morgan continued, "That's so crazy. What happened after that? Did you ever end up going to work for your mentor?"

# CHAPTER FIVE

## I Know What I Need to Do

AFTER A WONDERFUL evening, I went back to my apartment and continued to pack up the last of my belongings with the help of another one of my best friends, James Alvarez.

James and I first met in Dr. Roberts' sociology class at HSU. We were all freshmen, adapting to our new environment. For the day's lesson, Dr. Roberts was lecturing us about drugs and the effects each individual drug had on the human body. As I listened, I realized some of the information she had was wrong. I raised my hand, and Dr. Roberts acknowledged me.

She asked, "Roy, do you have a question?"

"No ma'am, I just want to say, that's not how drugs make you feel."

Her eyes opened wide and her eyebrows lifted. To our surprise, she made her way to the door, and shut it. She turned to face the class and in a slow, stern voice uttered, "Now class, this room is a safe environment to share. What is said in here, stays in here," she turned her head to look at me. "Roy, how do drugs make you feel?"

I looked to my right and left to see the entire class anticipating my answer. By the curious look on their faces, I knew then that my classmates and I did not have the same upbringing. I prefaced my comments with, "I don't use drugs… anymore… nor, will I ever again. I think they are stupid and will ruin your life. I was in a horrible place at the time and dealing with all kinds of childhood trauma. Now I know that there are smarter, healthier outlets for pain." After my disclaimer I continued to explain my experiences, and only one other guy in the room jumped into the conversation and shared his.

That evening, I was in the basement of the dorms, doing laundry, when the same guy walked in. I immediately recognized him because of his linebacker build, and spiky black hair. He reminded me of one of my cousins. When we finally made eye contact, he said, "Crazy class, huh?"

I laughed and agreed, then said, "Is it me or were there a lot of sheltered kids in there?"

"For real! I was thinking the same thing! Man, none of them understand real life."

"That's for sure. I'm Roy, by the way. I don't think I caught your name in class."

"I'm James. It's nice to meet you, Roy. Glad I found someone else in that class who gets it."

James and I became instant friends because of our similar backgrounds. Today he is my number one best friend. Yes, I have them numbered.

James is a part of my family and I am a part of his. His aunts JoAnn Alvarez and Jolisa Acevedo love to tease him by referring to me as their favorite nephew.

Now, three years after we first met, James was helping me pack and loading the small U-Haul. The next morning we left Abilene, Texas and headed for Las Vegas, Nevada where I would start my first job as a college graduate. A new chapter in my life was about to begin, and I couldn't wait to see what opportunities the future would hold for me.

Everything was happening so fast. I was heading to a new city, and I didn't even have a place to live. I asked my mentor if I could store my personal items in her garage and she didn't have an issue with it. She offered to let me sleep on her couch for as long as I needed but staying in her living room didn't make me feel like much of an adult. I knew we would be traveling for work the majority of the time, so I accepted her offer and gave myself a month to find an apartment or roommate.

One afternoon, as I was scrolling through my Facebook newsfeed, I noticed a post from my friend Nick, who lived in Vegas. It read: "I am looking for a roommate for my four-bedroom house. The house has a fireplace and a pool. Available immediately, let me know."

I thought, *This is awesome!* He knows a lot of people in Vegas, and I'm new in town. He seemed pretty cool from the past interactions we've had, but would I be able to live with him?

I was willing to give it a shot since I had been staying at my mentor's house for a few weeks and was eager to get off her couch. I responded to his message, writing, "What's up Nick? I just moved to Las Vegas, and I have been looking for a place to live. I just read your post about looking for a roommate. Here is a list of why I think I would make a great roommate:

1. I have a job and can pay my bills.
2. I am a clean person.
3. I am easy to get along with.
4. I am new in town so, I don't have ANY friends yet. You wouldn't have to worry about me having people over all the time. Hit me up and let me know what you think!"

About half an hour later, I received a reply from Nick. He explained that his house was much more beautiful than any apartment I was going to find, and I could stop by to see it anytime. The next day, I used MapQuest to look up the address he gave me. As I made my way to his house, I was excited about the possibility of finding a place to live. Sure enough, the house was beautiful and in a great location, only a fifteen-minute drive from work. All the neighbors' yards were well groomed, and the mountains in the distance provided a stunning view.

I walked up to the front door and rang the doorbell. I heard Nick yell from inside the house, "Come in!" I opened the door and stepped onto a polished, white tile floor. I could see the path it made from the front door all the way to the back of the house, where the living room was located. The walls were coated in a warm off-white and bare of any decorations. Still admiring the house as I walked towards the living room, Nick stood up from the dark brown couch.

"Hey man, what's up?" he said, greeting me.

"Hey Nick, how's it going?" I smiled.

"It's going pretty good. Welcome! This is the house," he said as he walked over to shake my hand. The house was nicer than what I had imagined. "Come over here, Roy; you haven't seen the best part of it yet."

We made our way back towards the living room. Off to the right of the living room was a large open kitchen with an island bar and five stools. All the appliances were stainless steel, and naturally, being a bartender, Nick had a Jäger machine that held three large bottles. I chuckled when I saw it. He looked back to me, "Nice huh? Check this out," he said as he made his way to the back-sliding door. He twisted open the patio door blinds to reveal an impressive Jacuzzi with a large waterfall pouring into it.

My eyes widened, "Wow!" I said, "That's awesome!"

He nodded in agreement; I could tell he was proud of the house. We stayed at the patio doors, staring at the water for a second until he broke the silence with, "Come on; let me show you the rooms."

He had just moved in himself, and three of the four bedrooms were still empty. "You can pick whichever room you like best. Once you decide, I plan to make the other two rooms into a weight room and a game room," he said with a huge smile.

He showed me each room, and I couldn't stop thinking how perfect everything seemed. To have the most privacy, I ended up choosing the furthest room from Nick's bedroom and said, "Man, if you are down, I am sold! I would love to move in!"

Without hesitation, he replied, "Let's do it Roy; you can move in now!"

## No Guarantees

The first three months working at EAS were great! I applied everything I learned in my internships and business classes. I arrived early, and left late, trying to figure out ways to bring more value to the company. However, I could sense something wasn't right with my mentor. As a small company, she had a lot on her plate. I figured she was under a lot of stress having to create enough wealth to sustain both payroll and her family. One morning, when I walked into the home office, early of course, Mrs. Kickbusch was sitting at the kitchen table when she called me over, "I need to speak with you."

I quickly grabbed a notepad and pen and asked how I could be of service.

She said, "I just want to let you know, you have three months left with my company, then I am going to let you go."

I was stunned. That was definitely not what I was expecting to hear. Confused, I asked, "Why? Are you not happy with my work? Is this something I can change?"

She responded sternly, "You don't get it, do you? You cannot work for me… If you work for me, you will never do what you are meant to do in life. You have three months to save money, and then I want you to go do what you are meant to do in life because I know you're not meant to stay working for me."

I was so confused, I had no idea what had just occurred. All I knew what I was terminated with a three-month warning.

I knew that I had to tell my new roommate. I had only been living with him for two weeks and I was still sleeping on the floor because I hadn't even bought furniture yet. I didn't know what I was going to do. Why would my mentor offer me a job only to let me go a couple of months later? Having to move from Texas to Las Vegas as a recent graduate wasn't easy or cheap. For a moment I thought that I should have just gone to the East Coast as I had planned, and none of this would have happened. I was having a hard time understanding the logic of my mentor's decision.

I came home from my meeting with Mrs. K, dreading the conversation I was about to have with Nick. One of the first things I told him before moving in was that I had a stable job and could afford rent. I felt horrible. When I got home, Nick was getting ready to leave for work. I slowly started the conversation, "Well… work sucked today."

"What? Why? What happened?"

There was no other way to tell him, so I just blurted it out, "I got fired today, but they are giving me a three-month notice."

He tilted his head to the side and slightly opened his mouth, as if to speak, but didn't say a word. Then came the question I was expecting, "So, what are you gonna do?"

There was a blank expression on my face. I had no clue what I was going to do, and that terrified me. But there was one thing I did know; I knew I was a survivor and I was going to figure this out.

Staying in Vegas without a job with my mentor seemed foreign. All the consolation Nick could offer was, "Damn man… that sucks…" and he was right. The situation sucked.

I decided then that I wasn't going to buy any furniture until I figured out what I was going to do. I asked my roommate if it was okay for me to sleep on his couch and he agreed, but only as long as he didn't have guests over. I told him I understood.

I alternated from the couch to the floor in my room then back to the couch. Every day that passed I found myself getting angrier. I wouldn't say I was mad at my mentor because I loved her, and I understood the stress she was under, but I was just frustrated at life. I thought graduating from college was going to be my "fix all." For once in my life, I believed everything was going to be okay, and now I felt that was the furthest from the truth.

You see, there are no guarantees in life for anyone. You have to work for what you want; you will always have to work. What my education gave me was options to live a better quality of life, but I was going to have to work hard, earn it, and maintain it.

One night, I came home from work, and it was rather late. I never worked conventional hours; most days I stayed in the office until 7:00 or 8:00 pm. Working for a small company, my job description was never really "defined"; so I learned to wear many hats, so to speak. It must have been a mixture of exhaustion, depression about losing my job, fear of the unknown, and utter frustration that made me feel like I was going to have a meltdown. Life had thrown me another curveball, and I had to figure out a way to overcome it. I grabbed my blanket from my room and laid down on the couch. As tears began to fall down my face, I whispered a plea, "God, what do you want from me? Please! What am supposed to be doing? I need your guidance, please." I prayed and prayed until I fell asleep.

That night, I had the most vivid dream. I can still recall this dream as though it had just happened.

In my dream, I stood outside a vast arena among a large crowd who were making their way into the building. As we entered, I could see how excited everyone was to be there. It was weird because it felt like no one could see me, but I was walking among everyone, watching everything unfold in real time. I could hear music and the crowd roaring from the foyer. I made my way to an opening and walked into the arena. The sight was amazing. There were people everywhere. The arena was filled from top to bottom, and I could feel the energy flowing. Balloons of all colors were being hit into the air by the crowd. On stage, a full band played as flashes of red, blue, green and purple lights illuminated the room. They repeatedly sang, "Come on in, come on in, together we can make a difference." The song still plays in my mind regularly.

Crowds were walking in by the hundreds, it felt as though we were at an international conference, where we were being equipped with the tools to fight social injustices throughout the world.

I jolted awake on the sofa, hearing the door slam. It was Nick, getting home from a shift. The clock on his entertainment center read 4:30 am. As I sat up, I realized there was no longer a feeling of sadness or confusion that filled me. It was as though my dream had given me clarity. With so much excitement in my voice, I shouted at him, "Nick, I know what I have to do!"

With both a surprised and confused look on his face, he asked, "What are you talking about?"

"A tour! I have to do a tour," I exclaimed as I ran around the house, packing things into my work bag.

"Now?" I heard off in the distance.

I laughed, "No, I'm not going to start the tour now… But I have to work. I have so much work to do."

With even more confusion in his voice, he asked, "Then where are you going?"

"To Denny's! I have to go to Denny's!" I yelled back to him as I ran out of the house. I drove to the closest Denny's which was about ten minutes away, on Tropicana Ave and Highway 215. I started to dream up what this tour would be like, it's mission. I had no clue where to start or how to do it, but I knew it had to be done.

Every morning after that, I would wake up super early and head to Denny's to work on the tour before I had to go to the office. Immediately after work, I would head back to the same Denny's and work on the tour until about 11:00 pm. My days began to merge into each other, and I never knew what day or time it was. This tour idea started to consume me.

One morning, I work up early, as usual, went to Denny's, then made my way to the office. As I walked past the kitchen, my mentor was in there making breakfast. She gave me a surprised look and asked, "What are you doing here?"

I was just as surprised at her question, "Uh, ma'am, with all due respect, I'm here to work."

She gave me a smirk and said, "Roy, it's Saturday."

We couldn't help but laugh with each other. I had been so consumed with planning my tour that I had no idea it was Saturday! I looked at her and said, "Well then, I'm here for breakfast! What are we having?"

She laughed and motioned me to have a seat at the empty table.

Mrs. K was more than a boss. She was my mentor and a second mother. I love this woman so much, and I believe she loves me just as much, which is why the discussion we were about to have would be mixed with a mother's love, a mentor's concern and a boss' ax.

With a stern voice, she began, "So, what's your plan, Roy?"

"Um, ma'am. I don't quite understand your question," I said, hoping for clarification.

"What is your plan?" she repeated. "You only have two months left with this company, and you haven't shown me your exit strategy."

"Mrs. Kickbusch," I started, "Can I share something with you? But, I want to share with you as my mentor and not my boss."

"Go ahead, tell me mijo," she said.

A bit nervous, I confessed, "I believe there is something I need to do." I stopped to take a deep breath. This was the first time I would share my idea, in detail, with anyone. "Every morning, I have been going to Denny's at about 5:00 am. When I leave work, I go back to the Denny's. I've been worki—" I stopped myself again. She gave me the look she always did when I was taking too long to get to the point. Finally, I shared, "I think I need to be homeless again."

My mentor looked at me, worried and confused, "What do you mean, mijo? Help me understand. Homeless?"

"Yes, Homeless. In two months, when my time with your company is over, I'm going to live out of my car and drive from Los Angeles, California to Jacksonville, Florida. It'll be like a tour," I smiled thinking about it. "My goal is to help kids like me. I want to reach them through my story, give them a chance to dream, a chance to be free. Just like you gave me a chance. I shouldn't be the only one to get this lucky."

My mentor smiled back at me, "Mijo, I'm truly proud of you for thinking of something like this. I know it's what you're meant to do. I love it and support you 100%." She paused for a brief second, then continued, "How can I help you? I can reach out to all my frien—"

"No!" I quickly interrupted. "I've seen how people take advantage of you, and I'm not gonna be one of them. I'll make my own contacts."

She nodded, "Thank you. I love you very much, Roy. You can do it."

I thanked her, then explained, "But what I do need your help with is figuring out what I'm gonna call the tour. What's a good name for what I'm trying to do? Will you help me think of something?"

We sat there over breakfast eating her famous pork chops and fried eggs and drank copious amounts of coffee, discussing a potential name. Everything we suggested just didn't seem to fit until finally, she said, "How about Homeless by Choice?"

"Homeless by Choice," I repeated. "Homeless by Choice. Yes! That's it, Mrs. K! The Homeless by Choice tour!"

## Planning the Tour and Saving

This was the first time I had ever planned a tour, so I had no clue where to start, nor did I have anyone to ask for advice. I knew that I wanted to cross the country and if I was going to visit schools, I had to work within their calendar. My first step would be to create a route and figure out a timeline.

I used MapQuest to generate a route from Los Angeles, California to Jacksonville, Florida. I slowly followed the path and wrote down every city I thought I could visit. Once I had all the cities written down, I pulled out a calendar and figured out how many days I could spend in each one. I decided I would allow three to four days in larger cities like San Diego, Las Vegas, or Phoenix and a day or a day and a half for the smaller ones like Deming, New Mexico, Sweetwater, Texas, or Pascagoula, Mississippi. I didn't want to leave out the smaller towns because I figured they probably rarely get to have national tours come through.

Next, I had to figure out where I would stay while on tour. I didn't mind sleeping in my car but figured I wouldn't want to do that every night. But then, a crazy idea struck me, and I decided to turn to my 700 friends on Facebook. I thought, *What if my friends could help me find places to sleep as I traveled?* I could make a post listing what cities I would be in and ask them to help me find a host family. Unsure if it would work, I decided to do a test run. To my surprise, I quickly had people respond to my post saying they would reach out to friends and relatives in the areas I had listed! Although this wasn't a guaranteed way to secure a place to stay, it appeared to be offering some hope.

As the days flew by and the tour was fast approaching, I began to panic. There was so much to do, and it all fell on top of me like a ton of bricks. There was only so much time to plan, research, organize, and send emails. For a majority of the week I was working from 5:00 am to midnight. I knew there was only so much money I could save in three months, and it wasn't enough for a national tour. Fear of the unknown and self-doubt began to set in. So many questions ran through my mind. *Who did I think I was trying to start a tour? What if I couldn't do it? What if I failed? What if I ran out of money in a city where I didn't know anyone?*

During this time a good friend of mine in Abilene, Texas had been messaging me, telling me how he wanted change in his life. When he said he wanted to, "go out and do something big," I saw this as a perfect time for a proposal.

I messaged him back and said, "Hey man, you want to be a part of a once-in-a-lifetime opportunity? Because, if you do, come to Vegas and join me on my national tour. I'm starting in a few weeks. The plan is to cross the country and inspire as many youths as possible." I was honest and told him I wasn't sure if I could pay him every couple of weeks like a typical job, but I would pay his bills while he joined me on tour and for his to move to Vegas.

The offer really peaked his interest, and he wanted to know more, so I called him to explain my dream and my vision in how to implement it. He was all in before I had even finished.

In less than a week, my good friend Allen packed up his things and began the long road trip from Abilene, Texas to Las Vegas, Nevada to join me. The night he arrived, I was extremely excited. Seeing him gave me the first feeling of *this is all happening*, and I was grateful that I wasn't going to have to go on tour alone. I felt comforted knowing that someone I trusted would be with me.

We hit the ground running. When Allen arrived, we worked on three different areas of the tour: schools, media, and sponsorship. We researched every alternative, middle and high school within a 3-hour drive of the cities chosen to be on the tour route. We also worked on media kits and press releases, hoping to get the word out. Finally, we reached out to every company you could imagine, hoping to get some type of sponsorship. Quickly, we learned that there was going to be even more work ahead of us than we had anticipated.

On average we sent out about 600 emails a day just to get 3 responses each time. The responses weren't even confirmed speaking events; they were more of a, "tell us more about it, and we will let you know." When it came to sponsorship, every single door was closed to us. The fact that we couldn't get any sponsors really discouraged me. I had just promised Allen that I could pay his bills, and I had only saved a little under two-thousand dollars for the tour, so I wasn't sure how I was going to make this happen without sponsors.

## The Crash

A month before the tour was launched, I had agreed to be the best man at my friend's wedding. I was excited and honored to have been asked to be a part of such a symbolic ceremony, but I have to be honest; in the back of my mind,

I thought about how expensive it was going to be. I thought about how I was going to have to rent a tuxedo, purchase a plane ticket, get a rental car, and stay in a hotel. Because I was funding the Homeless by Choice tour with my own money, I would have to use some of the money I had been saving for the tour to be a part of this special ceremony. After putting much thought into it, I realized, *I can't just exist in life. I need to live life.* It's not every day one of your best friends gets married; I'd just have to work a little harder to replace the funds I was going to use.

Two weeks before the tour, I left Vegas and flew to New Orleans, Louisiana where my friend, Jennifer O'Sullivan, had agreed to pick me up and drive me to the wedding in Biloxi, Mississippi. The wedding was absolutely beautiful, it was held at St. Alphonsus Catholic Church in Ocean Springs, Mississippi.

While at the wedding reception, my phone began vibrating. I looked down, and noticed it was Allen, my traveling assistant. It was a weird time to call, because it was midnight his time. It was 2:00 am here, and the wedding party was still going strong.

I walked away to a place where I could talk.

Immediately Allen began saying, "I'm so sorry, I'm so sorry."

In a stern but curious voice, I asked, "Allen, what are you sorry about?"

"I'm sorry Roy, I'm so sorry," he repeated himself.

In an authoritative tone, I asked again, "Allen, what are you sorry about?"

Alan took a deep breath. He paused for a second. I waved my hand as if to hurry him up like I was there with him. He spoke tentatively, "Roy, I took your car out to the Vegas strip, and someone crashed into your car…"

At that moment, I'm not too sure if he kept talking or not because my mind had completely disconnected from the conversation. My heart sank into my stomach because I didn't know what I was going to do. The tour was starting in two weeks, and I knew that the little money I had saved was now going to have to be used to fix my car which would leave nothing for the tour.

In my mind, I kept asking myself, *Roy, what would Mrs. K do?* Then it hit me; she would make this a teachable moment. I said, "Allen, the car can be fixed, but what you did tonight was break my trust. Why would you take my car out to the strip when you have your own truck? You know what? It doesn't matter, we'll deal with this when I get back. I am glad you're okay, have a good night."

I hung up the phone and tried to enjoy the rest of the wedding. However, it was downhill from there because that night, I also lost my cell phone. When it rains, it pours, right?

When I got back to Vegas, the first thing I did was examine my car to see what damage had been done. It was worse than I imagined. The entire back was wrecked! The trunk wouldn't close, parts of the bumper were missing, and it was definitely going to need a paint job. I stood there staring at my car, trying not to be upset at Allen for taking it out. *What was I going to do now? How was I going to afford to fix the car with the tour only a week away?* Luckily, my friend Jesús was a mechanic, who would give me a good deal, so I took my car to him.

As Jesús examined my red bumper, almost hanging to the ground, he asked, "Como paso esto?" (How did this happen?)

I gave Allen a side eye, and replied, "He hit a pole."

Jesús laughed, "Yo puedo arreglarlo." (I can fix it).

Unfortunately, he'd have to order in all the parts and paint because the shop didn't have them.

"Okay, that's fine. How long will that take?" I asked, knowing I'd more than likely have to put fixing my car on hold.

In his thick Spanish accent, and his best English, he replied, "Necesitar un week. I buy el paint y partes first. Then days for me to work. I say, two weeks and it's done."

I tried not to appear devastated; I didn't have two weeks to wait. I couldn't put the tour on hold for my car to get fixed. I stood with the mechanic in silence for a moment.

He noticed the stress in my face and tried to ease my frustration by saying, "I can try for a week and a half."

I took a deep breath.

I knew he was trying to help, but it still wouldn't fix my problem. I was supposed to start my national tour in a week and I needed my car.

"Thanks man," I said, still trying to figure out a solution, "But... you know what? That won't really work for me either. Could I just pay you for the parts now and come back in two weeks to have the car fixed? I can't put off the work I have lined up. Plus, when I come back, I'll be in town for a week before I leave again, that should be enough time to work on it, right?"

He looked at me and then looked back at the car.

"Sí puedo. I get the parts and get the car fixed antes que te vayas," he replied.

A small weight lifted off my shoulders, at least I had figured out how to fix the car without causing any delays to the tour. I reluctantly handed over the tour money I had been saving up—$1,000—to pay the mechanic to order all the parts.

Allen and I packed the car with everything we thought we'd need for the tour and started our trip. The drive from Vegas to Los Angeles is only around four hours long, but I have to admit, those were some of the longest hours of my life. With only $16 to my name, doubts swarmed my head. I didn't have any money! I was driving around with a broken car and the stress of how I would pay for the tour. In addition, paying our bills was weighing on my mind. I was starting to doubt my plan. As we approached L.A., things didn't seem to get any better. A light drizzle started, and within an hour, it got heavier with every mile we drove further into the city. Turns out L.A. was about to experience some of the most severe thunderstorms it had seen in decades. So instead of stopping anywhere to explore, Allen and I drove straight to our first host family's house. For the tour, I accepted any family, person, or organization that was willing to host me, the majority of them I didn't know personally.

When we showed up to our first house, we called to let them know we were outside, but no one answered. *No worries,* I thought, *I'll just call again in a couple of minutes.* Still sitting in the car with Allen, I called a second time, and still no answer. An hour passed and I called again; this time it went straight to voicemail. We were tired and frustrated, so we began talking about what our options were. At first, Allen and I decided we were going to sleep in the car until the morning. It seemed like a good idea until we realized the rain wasn't going to let up and all our things were in the trunk... the broken trunk that wouldn't close all the way. So, to waste some time, we drove to the closest Denny's because we knew it'd be open 24 hours.

For a while, we sat in the parking lot of Denny's trying to figure out what we were going to do if the host family didn't call back. Allen and I agreed, if we had to, we'd sleep in our car in the parking lot. Just as we made up our minds that we'd be sleeping in the car, my phone rang; it was the host family! The man, Mr. Romero, called us back half an hour later. In a monotone voice, he apologized for not answering our calls and asked if we'd still like to stay.

I replied, "It's not a problem sir, my assistant and I will head that way now. Thank you."

We were relieved that they called back! It felt so much better that we had the chance to stay in a house rather than in my car, especially on our first night! When we got to their house, the Romero's showed us to their sons' bedroom where Allen and I would sleep. Thankfully, there were two beds so neither of us would have to sleep on the floor.

The next day, the rain came down like there was no tomorrow, but despite the weather, I was anxious to start the tour. As usual, the first thing I did was check my emails. To my dismay, I had received emails from three different schools canceling the event due to the weather. *Just my luck,* I thought. The first three events on tour had been canceled. Therefore, we would be leaving the host family's house with no money and no place to stay. Allen and I gathered up our things and packed them to continue with our journey.

"Thank you all so much for having Allen and me. We really appreciate it; you have a lovely home," I said as we headed out to leave.

"Oh, thank you Roy! Good luck on your tour this week, we hope the best for you," Mrs. Romero replied.

I forced a smile but couldn't help but admit to her that the first week would be slow due to all the cancellations I received because of the weather.

"That's terrible! Why don't you... hm... Wait right here," she said as she walked back to her bedroom. I could hear her talking to her husband from the living room but didn't know what they were saying. Allen was still walking in and out of the house, loading our stuff into our broken trunk, (Cough,

cough, thanks Allen!) when they came out of the room.

"Roy, I'm told that your week's events are canceled," Mr. Romero said.

"Yes sir, I just opened my email this morning and read the messages. So, I guess we'll just be starting up next week instead. We weren't expecting such heavy rain," I tried to play off how disappointed I was.

"Well Roy, I know I didn't answer and kept you and Allen waiting yesterday, so I want to make it up to you. If you'd like, you can come to the school I work at, I'm not sure if I could get you a large crowd, but maybe a classroom or two if you're willing," he offered.

I knew it wouldn't be many students that would hear my message but being able to reach out to one person was better than none. "I'd love to sir. Anything would help at this point." I thanked him with a nod and a soft smile.

"Perfect. You guys can follow me to work!"

# CHAPTER SIX

## Sharing a Hot Tea

W E FOLLOWED MR. ROMERO to Ouchi High School which was in South Central, Los Angeles, and known to be one of the toughest areas of the city due to its high crime rate. Since my first three events were canceled, this was going to be my first speaking engagement on tour, and my nerves were building as we pulled into the parking lot. I was surprised they didn't cancel school because it was still pouring outside. We quickly ran into the school to avoid getting drenched. Once inside he led us to a classroom.

"I called a couple of my colleagues on the way over here, and one of them agreed to let you speak," Mr. Romero said, standing outside the classroom door. "Let me inform her you're here, and then you can come on in," he continued as we walked through the doorway, closing the door behind him.

I stood in the hallway with sweat beads dripping down my forehead. Although I knew it was going to be a small class, this would be my first time telling my story on tour.

I saw the doorknob turn, and Mr. Romero peeked his head into the hallway, "Okay Roy, come on in!"

I walked into the classroom trying not to show my nervousness. About 15 to 20 students were sitting at their desks, staring at me unenthusiastically. I didn't even get a chance to meet the teacher when she began introducing me, "Alright everyone, we have a guest speaker. I want you to treat him with the utmost respect. Do not talk while he's talking, or I will have you do work out in the hall." She then turned to me and said, "Welcome sir, the floor is yours."

I smiled and introduced myself to the students, "Hey guys, my name is Roy Juarez Jr., but before I start, I first want to thank your teacher for allowing me to come in here and share my story with you. A story about how at the age of 14, I ended up homeless on the streets of San Antonio…"

I did my very best to inspire the students with my presentation, but I was still piecing together what my message would be and how I would tell my story. Regardless, I poured my heart out, and once I finished, I knew I had struck a chord with some of them. They began asking me questions about my life and my family for the next 15 minutes before I had to go. Just as I was about to leave, a slender young man, about 5'9" (my height), approached me. Before I had the chance to say anything, he said, "Aye sir, I need to talk to you."

His angry tone caught me off guard.

"Yes mijo, of course. Did you enjoy my presentation?" I asked, wondering if I had said something that offended him.

"Nah. Come here." He demanded.

Concerned, I asked, "Hey, we're cool, right?"

He ignored my question and repeated himself as he walked towards the door, away from the other students, "Come here."

Once we were out in the hallway, away from everyone else, I tried to ask him what was going on. He cut me off mid-sentence, "That story you told… man, is it even true?"

I replied, "Yeah man, it is true."

He looked at me skeptically and continued, "I'm asking you sir. I'm asking you because your story is my story. So, is it true?"

Again I replied, "Yes, mijo, it's true."

He stepped back, and in an attempt to prove I was dishonest, he asked, "Alright, then. I only have one question for you. How are you banking off this?"

When I heard him ask that question, I knew he wasn't really asking how much money I was making to be there. His question was much deeper than that. I could tell by the anger in his voice and the way his hands clenched the straps of his backpack. This kid was hurt and I suspected he had learned not to trust people. I'm sure that he wanted to believe my words about never giving up, and that life would get better, but he first needed to know if I was there for him or if I was there to make money.

While it would have been perfectly okay to get paid for my time, efforts, and experience, this wasn't the reason I was on this tour, and I'm glad that it wasn't. I knew exactly where this kid was coming from. I looked at him and saw myself.

I remember the first family who took me in from the streets when I was just fourteen years old. They welcomed me with open arms, but there was always that feeling in the pit of my stomach that I didn't belong. A different family once told me I could make myself at home, but the next moment, they restricted what I was allowed to eat from their refrigerator. The next family told me they cared so much about me and that I was "one of the family," but I wasn't allowed to have their cell number because only their children were allowed to have it. Other families would say, "Roy, we love you like a son" and there was such a huge desire in my heart to be a part of a family that I believed them.

I especially felt loved when my fifteenth birthday came and the family I was living with started my morning with a "Happy Birthday Roy!" In my mind, I couldn't believe it. This family had cared enough to actually remember my birthday when my own family didn't even care enough to know where I was. I thought, *Wow, they do love me like a son.* But that feeling was short lived.

Two weeks later, when their birth son had a birthday, they didn't just wish him a "happy birthday." They celebrated his big day with a cake decorated with candles, presents that were wrapped, and balloons which read *Birthday Boy.* When I saw all this, something clicked in my mind: They didn't love me like a son. Those were just words they were telling me, empty words. Maybe I should have been grateful to this family for giving me a roof over my head and food on my plate, but I was young, and I didn't know how to deal with what I was feeling. I felt hurt, betrayed, alone, and lied to. It felt like every family who took me in would eventually hurt me because they didn't really care.

The next family that took me in said the same thing as all the others, but I was already jaded. I figured none of them really wanted me, it was just an adult's way of trying to make me feel accepted by them. Once again, I heard them say, "Roy, we love you like a son."

From that moment, I always replied to that statement instinctively with, "Naw, you don't. You don't love me like a son, trust me."

The family after that used the same line again. Almost every family who used that line eventually asked me to leave. They all got tired of having me as a "son." I wasn't able to handle it anymore. I started building walls to keep people out because I was afraid they'd hurt me. I was so tired of being hurt.

Standing in front of me was a hurt young man. I was able to recognize the behavior he exhibited because it was so familiar to me. I made an effort to be as transparent as possible with him, saying, "I'm gonna be honest; whether you wanna believe me or not is up to you, mijo. Basically, I tried to get sponsors for this tour, but everyone I've reached out to either told me no or didn't even bother to respond to my emails or the messages I left when I called. If you want to know the truth, I'm not getting paid to be here, I only have $16 in my pocket, and I have no idea where I'm gonna sleep tonight."

He looked at me, eyes wide, and asked, "For real sir?"

And I replied, "Yes, for real."

"Wow sir. That's awesome. Man, that's so awesome, sir," his shoulders fell a few inches as he released the grip on his backpack straps and slipped me a smile. He leaned in, gave me a huge hug, and said, "Thank you, Sir. Thank you for coming today; it means a lot," before he walked away.

I stood there in awe. I wasn't sure what had just happened but clearly something important did. The difference in that young man's face and demeanor changed something in me. It made me think, *Maybe I don't need any sponsors.* Perhaps it was a good thing all those companies and organizations told me no because I didn't want anything to come between my message and the students. That day, I decided to stop looking for sponsors. I thought, *How hard could it be? I've been homeless before.*

My new plan was to survive off the generosity of the communities I served. To save on cost, my traveling assistant and I decided to couch surf the entire tour. I was sure I could get the community to help me. I thought it'd be relatively straightforward. Boy was I wrong.

## I Never Said I was Quitting

After I finished speaking, Allen and I had nowhere to go. It was only 10:00 am and our next host family wasn't going to be home until 6:00 pm. We decided we would just drive to the area where they lived and wait around. Since we weren't familiar with California, we didn't pay much attention to how close our host families were to each other. We were just concerned with finding a place to sleep for the night. I typed the address into my GPS for the next house and was shocked to see the drive was over an hour long. With only $16 left, I was able to get almost five gallons of gas which would give up about 95 miles. Now the tour didn't have any money, and we were off to Chino Hills, California.

Once we were close enough to the house, we stopped at the nearest Starbucks to pass the time. This was before Starbucks offered free Wi-Fi, so if you wanted to use their Wi-Fi, there was a $20 monthly fee that needed to be paid. Luckily, I had already paid for the month. Knowing how long we'd be waiting there, Allen started looking for loose change in the car, so we could buy something. He found about $2 worth of change, which wasn't much, but it was enough to buy a hot tea for the both of us to share.

We sat there in silence and I went on Facebook to post about how things were going on the tour. I had promised my family and friends I wouldn't just post the highs, but I would also post the lows. I wanted everyone to feel as though they were on this journey with me, and I wanted to write it as authentically as possible. In my post, I wrote about how I felt like a failure because my first three events were canceled due to the rain storms. I also wrote about how Allen and I were now sharing a $1.95 hot tea. I didn't feel great writing the post, but it was cathartic once I finished it.

Almost immediately after I made the post public, I received a notification that someone made a comment. It was from an ex-coworker, who I had heard was making bets behind my back on how long I would last on tour. His comment read, "Well, you tried. Now have a nice drive home."

This really pissed me off.

I replied, "I never said I was quitting. I mentioned before I started the tour that I was going to share the highs and the lows, but I NEVER said I was quitting."

I was fuming, I couldn't believe the audacity of his comment, but I wasn't surprised. Just as I went to log out of Facebook, I saw my host family had sent me a private message:

"Hey Roy. I wanted to let you know that I didn't go to work today. I'm home! Please feel free to come over whenever you're ready. —Aurora Kamimura"

As soon as I finished reading the message I said to Allen, "Bro, our host family is home! Let's pack up."

I quickly replied to Aurora, "Thank you so much, we're on our way."

I wanted to get to her house as quickly as possible because it was still raining, and our clothes were still in the trunk. Once we arrived, Aurora walked out of her house and greeted us with a warm smile and a huge embrace. Her beautiful auburn curls quickly fell from the weight of the rain.

As we all ran back inside, I asked her, "Aurora, everything in our trunk is wet! Do you mind if we do some laundry here?"

"Oh no! Of course you can do your laundry," she said.

Aurora was extremely accommodating. She even helped us take everything out of my trunk.

Suddenly I heard Allen say, "Hey Roy, you rest; I will take care of all this laundry."

He was probably still feeling bad about wrecking my car, so I didn't put up much of a fight to stop him. Despite everything, I am so glad we are still close friends to this day.

We had a great night with the Kamimura family. They fed us well, we laughed, and we now had clean, dry clothes! The best part was, Allen and I had a place to sleep. As I laid there on their couch that evening, I had so many thoughts running through my mind. I would be lying to you if I said I wasn't scared. I was terrified of the unknown. I asked myself, *Roy, what did you get yourself into?* I said my bedtime prayers and begged God to please, please open the right doors for us.

The next morning, we woke up to a delicious home-cooked breakfast, which tasted even better as we had no money to buy food. As we were getting ready to leave, Aurora's husband, Dr. Mark Kamimura said, "Roy I want to give you something before you leave."

It caught me by surprise because I wasn't expecting anything; they had already given us more than enough. He handed me a book entitled, *The Latina/o Pathway to the Ph.D.* At first, I wasn't sure why he gave me this book. I had just finished my bachelors and I am so far away from a Ph.D., but then I noticed that his name was on the cover.

I said, "Oh wow, this is your book! Thank you so much!"

He replied, "Not a problem. I even signed it for you."

I thanked him and gripped the book tightly towards my chest. I walked out the door and began helping Allen load the car with all our clean clothes. We weren't in a hurry, but I had found a Kiwanis Club in Burbank, California that was meeting and I figured it would be a great way to connect with people and share our mission.

Kiwanis Club is an international organization with over 600,000 members in more than 80 countries. Each club meets and addresses the needs of the youth in their community. I was aware of the Kiwanis because I was a member of one of their clubs while in college. I decided to show up to their meeting and ask the president if I could have 5 minutes to share information about the Homeless by Choice tour. I was hoping that they would be able to get us into a local school.

Driving to Burbank, we tried keeping our minds away from planning what we'd do next. You would think planning would be essential for the tour, right? Well, with a nickel to our names, we decided to take things one step at a time. It wasn't until after we left, that I realized how far the meeting was from our host family's house. The trip was going to consume most of our gas. The meeting was being held at the Burbank Community YMCA. As we pulled into the parking lot with my car starved of gas, my stomach started to turn. I was nervous and excited.

Allen must have seen the nervousness in my face because just before we got out of the car, he placed his hand on my shoulder and reassured me, "You got this, man. I wouldn't be here if I didn't believe in you. You got this."

I gave a half smile, not really believing things were going to work out.

"Thanks Allen; it means a lot," I replied.

When we got inside, I asked the first person I saw where the president might be. The lady looked at me confused, "The president isn't here today, but you can talk with me. My names Cynthia," she said.

"Oh hi, Cynthia, I'm Roy Juarez Jr. from Texas."

Her face lit up, "No way! I'm from Texas, too! Please call me Cynthia Ann! What're you doing out here?"

I shared with her the journey we were about to take and asked her, "Do you mind if I share a bit about the tour with everyone? Maybe five minutes of your time?"

"Of course, come on in and let me introduce you to everyone."

I followed her into the room where the meeting was being held. Right before it began, Allen and I took a seat. Our new friend Cynthia Ann walked to the front to welcome everyone.

"Good afternoon everyone. Thank you for joining in today's meeting. We have two young men here, from Texas, who are starting something amazing. We're going to give them five minutes of floor time to share with everyone what they're doing. Roy, come on up here," she announced.

I walked slowly towards where she was standing, still unsure of myself and the tour's future. Not really knowing what to say to this group of business owners and community leaders, I just began sharing my story of growing up as a homeless teenager and how that eventually led to my vision of the Homeless by Choice tour. As I finished speaking, she came back up and said, "Now isn't that amazing? You know what? I think we should take up an offering for these young men. Will someone get a basket going around, so we can start that up? Thank you."

Allen and I looked at each other in total surprise because we didn't have any money! I couldn't believe the members were actually reaching in their pockets to donate; they didn't even know us! My heart started to beat so fast, and I felt this wave of peace come over me. God must have had heard my prayers, and it was all going to be okay.

At the end of the meeting, Cynthia Ann came over to me and handed me the offering; they had collected $181. I gave her the biggest hug and thanked her. She had no idea how much her gesture had done for us, and how much she helped keep the tour alive.

I looked at Allen and said, "We're back on the map; we can do this!"

He replied, "I told you; I wasn't worried."

We both laughed, and I said, "You're such a liar; you were just as nervous as I was."

It was amazing, a miracle. Ecstatic to share the news, I rushed to log in to Facebook. But before I was able to update my status, I noticed my friend, Lisa Cummins—the President of Urban Strategies—was in Los Angeles from Washington, D.C. When I saw her post, I turned to Allen and said, "We have to go there! She's in a meeting, and I know they're going to have food!"— Who could turn down free food?

Walking into the meeting, we saw Lisa right away. Of course, she looked at me, surprised. She asked, "Roy? What are you doing here?"

"I saw that you were in town, so I thought I'd stop by," I said, telling half the truth.

"I'm so glad you stopped by. Are you guys hungry? Do you want something to eat?"

Allen and I glanced over at each other, eyes wider than usual, and chuckled. I replied, "We'd love something to eat Lisa; thank you."

While we ate, I told her more about what I was doing out in California, and halfway through our conversation, she asked, "Roy! You know I have about 80 nonprofits from all over the L.A. area in this room, right? You want five minutes with them to share what you're doing?"

"Oh my gosh Lisa, please! I would love that. Are you sure it's okay?"

She nodded and said, "Finish eating, and then I will introduce you."

A few minutes later, Lisa interrupted their meeting and said, "I have a colleague who is in town, and I would like to give him five minutes to share his journey. Roy, come up here and share it with everyone."

I got up on stage and shared my vision with the audience. After I was done speaking, I stayed until the meeting was over and talked to Lisa and several organization leaders.

I was so thankful Lisa allowed me to share my journey with individuals who could possibly help me reach more students. As Allen and I walked to our car through what was now just drizzle, one lady stopped us in the parking lot. She reached out to shake my hand and placed something covertly in my palm, "Hi, I'm Tabitha. It's great to hear what you're doing, and I know how hard things must be. I wish you both the best. Thank you for stopping by today."

"Thank you so much Tabitha. And thank you for having us," I replied.

She walked away, and I placed what she gave me in my pocket, so it didn't get wet. Then a second lady approached us and said, "Hi, my name is Dianne. I don't have any money to donate to your tour, but I do own a Bed & Breakfast in Beverly Hills. If you guys don't have a place to stay this evening, you're more than welcome stay the night."

Alan and I looked at each other with dropped jaws.

I looked back at Dianne and grabbed both of her hands as I said, "Oh my God! Thank you so much!"

I released her hands because I noticed her body tense up. I continued, "We actually don't have a place to stay tonight. We would really appreciate it." We exchanged contact information then she walked back into the building.

For a moment, I felt relieved. We had a place to stay for the night and $181. I looked at my phone and noticed I had a missed call from Dr. Mark Kamimura. I looked over at Allen, "Hey, Dr. Mark called. Did you forget anything at their house?" I asked.

"No, I don't think so. We should have everything. I double checked the rooms and the restroom," Allen explained.

"You didn't take their car out to the strip and crash it did you?" I started laughing.

"You're a jerk!" Allen replied.

"Well, I'll call him back when we get in the car to make sure everything's okay. Can you look up a gas station on the GPS? We need to fill up."

We hopped into the car and turned to each other, grinning.

I said, "Wow, what a day it's been so far man!"

Allen replied, "See Roy, I told you things we're gonna be okay!"

"Yeah man, I feel like things are turning around! But I don't want to get my hopes up just yet. Kind of seems too good to be true… Anyway, I don't know if you saw, but that lady slipped something into my hand," I said as I pulled out a folded-up piece of paper. It was a check! I quickly unfolded it and scanned my eye across the text. "Allen… it's a check is for $300!"

"What?" he shouted.

"$300!" I exclaimed, pointing to the check. I couldn't believe it. Allen turned up the volume on the radio and "Dynamite" by Taio Cruz was playing. He started dancing with excitement. Ecstatic about what had just happened, I joined in the celebration and started dancing along with him. This didn't last long before a gentleman walked passed our car, staring at us as though we were crazy.

"Oh damn, for a second I thought that was Dr. Mark!" Allen said.

"Crap, I forgot to call Dr. Mark!"

"Hey, maybe with our new luck, he's going to ask us to stay again! They had a really nice house," Allen said laughing.

I dialed Dr. Mark's number, and he answered quickly, "Hello?"

"Hey Mark, it's Roy Juarez Jr. I saw that I had a missed call from you, so I was just returning your call to make sure everything was okay," I replied.

"Everything's fine Roy. I was just wondering if you were able to take a look at my book," I looked at Allen confused. I had briefly opened the book, but did he expect me to have already read some of it?

"Oh, yes sir. I saw you signed it and I looked over it, but I haven't had time to read it yet," I said nervously.

Then I heard him laugh on the other end, "No Roy, have you checked the flap of the book?"

"Oh… no, I haven't. Hold on…" I covered my phone and looked at Allen. "He said to look in the flap of the book; hurry get it!" I whispered.

Allen grabbed the book, opened the flap, and $100 fell out. We looked at each other, nodded, and silently started to do our celebration dance again.

I collected myself, and put the phone up to my ear again, "I just opened the flap, and I can't thank you and Aurora enough. Letting us stay in your home was already too kind, but this gesture just throws it over the top."

"It was a pleasure, and we wanted to be able to do more for the cause. You're going to do great things Roy."

His words put a huge smile on my face.

We spoke for a brief moment longer and then ended the call. With tears beginning to fill my eyes, I looked down at the check we had just been given and the $100. Within hours, we went from having absolutely nothing for the tour, to having been blessed with $581. I already felt like things were going to get better after we received the $181, but now I knew everything on the tour was going to be okay.

It was after 8:00 pm when we finally made it to our next host family, Mr. John Lewis, who lived in Alhambra, California. We arrived and could see him through his living room window, sitting at his desk. I was surprised by how young he looked. I was expecting an older, heavy-set man, which was the opposite of Mr. Lewis. He was a slender man about 35, with 5 o'clock shadow. From the street, I called him and watched as he answered the phone.

I said, "Mr. Lewis, we've arrived. I'm the gentleman staring at you through your window!"

I guess that wasn't the best way to introduce myself to someone who I had never met before, especially as I was about to stay the night in their house! Despite how creepy I must have come across, Mr. Lewis was very welcoming when he greeted us outside and insisted we called him John. As we had dinner with John that evening, we learned what a great man he is. He was doing a lot of work in the community, focusing on fatherhood issues and training people around the country on how to write grants.

Our sleeping arrangements were a bit different from our last host family. We had our own places to sleep. I called shotgun on the couch in the living room. Allen slept in John's 7-year-old son's room! He decided to turn in before John and me. When I was ready to go to bed, I had to move my car from the street and park it in the driveway. Allen was trying in vain to sleep when I got my car keys off him, but he didn't know how to turn off the bedroom light, which I'm sure didn't help. He reverted back to his childhood days and used the Ninja Turtles blankets to build a fort in order to block out the light. I thought it was hilarious, so I took a picture.

# CHAPTER SEVEN

## The Night Grew Darker

### San Diego, California - 1 Month into the Tour

THE TOUR STARTED to pick up momentum as more and more people heard about what Allen and I were doing. With all the buzz going around, we received an invitation to speak for Monarch Schools in San Diego, California. I was ecstatic and decided to research what the school would be like. When I visited their website, I was surprised to learn Monarch Schools exclusively serviced homeless youth. I had never heard of a school with its entire population made up of homeless students! I knew this presentation was going to be difficult. I would be sharing a story that every student was currently living, and I needed to make sure that I was sensitive, sympathetic, and caring towards their situation.

Scrolling through Monarch's website, I came across their mission: The mission of the Monarch School is to educate students impacted by homelessness and to help them develop hope for a future with the necessary skills and experiences for personal success.

I read the mission statement to Allen and said, "I hope we can be a part of that mission. This one is going to be a tough one."

When the day finally arrived, I felt anxious as we walked into the school. I knew every student that passed by me was homeless and could relate to my story. The students weren't phased by my presence and kept about their business as we passed each other in the hallways. We checked in at the front office where the Vice Principal, Mr. Garcia, was waiting to greet us. He gave us a tour of the school and shared how their schedule worked. At the time, they opened up at 6:00 am to provide breakfast for the students and their family, then closed really late to provide dinner.

After the tour of the school, he led us to the classroom where I would give my presentation. As we stood outside the classroom door, we watched the students working. It looked like every other classroom from the outside, but these students weren't like any other students, they were living a tough life. If it was anything like mine, they knew domestic violence, neglect, and hunger. I could only imagine what they might be going through. I flashed back to the domestic violence my siblings and I had endured; the violence that would eventually lead me to become a homeless teenager and would have secured me a seat in that classroom.

***

"SHUT UP! Just shut the hell up!" my father yelled. I could hear my mother begging him to leave her alone when he yelled again, "You want to talk to me like that? You think you're going to tell me to get out?"

I squeezed into bed between my two older sisters, Amy and Tammy. We laid in the dark, listening to our parents argue in the next room. It had become routine for them to try and comfort me, but I could never shake the feeling of fear that ran through my body.

In a frightened voice, my mother pleaded, "Okay… okay, I'm sorry just stop. Please!" there was a quick moment of silence before she started screaming, "STOP! Rogelio stop! You're hurting me! Stop!"

Her cries tore through the walls, and I swear for a moment we were all in the same room. Her voice was clear, "Just stop it, please stop it," she continued to plead, "Baby Amy! Baby Amy come here! Please hurry, come here!"

"Shut up," my father yelled again.

My sister Amy laid next to me, with tears in her eyes. We all flinched when a thump echoed through the house. This time, the noise was accompanied by what sounded like a loud cracking noise, followed by silence. I sat up.

"Mom?" I tried to call out through the door which was only a couple of feet away.

"Lay down Roy," my sister Tammy said in a whisper, "Don't get up! Stay right here! You don't wa—" she stopped talking when another banging sound came through the wall.

"What's happening Tammy? What's going on?" I begged my sister to tell me when the sound of my mother's voice faded out my own.

"Rogelio, get off me! Stop it! Baby Amy, please help me!" she screamed.

My siblings and I laid in the darkness. Tears rolled down our faces as we heard one last slamming sound followed by silence. I could feel my heart thumping in my throat. I stayed deathly still hoping to hear that everything was okay. What had just happened? Why was my mother screaming? Was she hurt?

The door to our room swung open. The light from the living room flooded the darkness out of our bedroom. Filling the doorway was my father's silhouette.

"Where's mom?" I sat up and asked.

"Don't worry about it, go back to bed," he demanded. He slammed the door and as quickly as the light entered the room it was gone, leaving my sisters and me afraid and confused.

The next morning, I awoke to the sun creeping into my room through the window. I rubbed my puffy eyes and tip-toed over to the bedroom door. As I reached for the doorknob, my heart was racing, and I noticed that my palms were sweaty. My body had not shaken the fear from the night before. Taking a deep breath, I turned the knob and pulled the door open only an inch, to check cautiously what was on the other side. I peeked through the crack in the door. To my surprise, my sisters were watching cartoons with my dad. Everything seemed "normal"; however, my mother was nowhere to be found, and I was too scared to ask where she was.

I can't recall which one of us told my dad we were hungry, but the topic was brought up. My siblings and I agreed cereal would be a perfect breakfast. The only problem was we didn't have any milk. We started searching for something else to eat when my father called out from the living room. "Y'all want cereal? Well come on, let's go get some milk."

We all loaded the car to head for the corner store. Amy and Tammy ran in to get the milk with some money my father given them, and we headed back to the apartment.

Pulling in the complex, I counted the building numbers in my head, 1… 3… 4… We lived towards the back of the complex, so our building wasn't visible from the street. 10…13… My counting was interrupted when my father slammed on the breaks. I turned my attention from the building numbers to our apartment building. There were two cop cars parked with their red and blue lights flashing.

Off in the distance, I could see my mother looking our way, pointing to us, as one of the men in blue approached our car holding on to his thick black belt. He looked so serious, his face was expressionless when he said with a deep voice, "Sir, I need you to put the car in park and turn off the ignition," the officer instructed through the window. My father didn't say a word as he obliged.

The cop continued, "Are you Rogelio sir?"

"Yes sir I am," my father replied.

"Okay sir, I'm going to need you to please step out of the vehicle," he instructed again.

My father unbuckled his seatbelt and got out. Then he and the cop walked to the rear of the car. Not sure of what was going on, my sisters and I quickly looked at each other with worry. Too young to fully understand the situation, all my sisters and I could do was watch their conversation through the back window. We were unable to hear what they were saying, but I could see my father staring straight at my mother. The look he was giving her woke something inside me, something that had never been there before.

Suddenly, I could hear my mother in the distance. When I turned to look at her, I noticed she was carrying a huge trash bag. She opened the driver door and threw it in the back seat next to me. I waited for her to get in the car with us but then she turned around, and a cop escorted her back into our apartment. Confused, I peeked inside the bag she had thrown next to me. It was filled with clothes. I looked back up to search for my mother and saw her walking over to us with more belongings in her arms.

"I guess she's getting whatever she can…" Tammy whispered to Amy as my mom walked towards us.

"Buckle up kids, let's go," my mother said as she got into the car. I watched her turn the key in the ignition and realized she was wearing the same clothes from the night before. But her makeup was different, she had painted a black circle around one of her eyes.

The cop who had escorted her back and forth lingered by the driver's window before warning us to be careful. This wasn't the first time I had seen a man in that uniform. I had seen it worn before by a woman who had stopped by my house when my parents were arguing, but I was much younger then. Perhaps it was because I was a little older that made this visit different from all the others, but this scene is ingrained in my memory and the sounds embedded in my mind. The man standing in the dark uniform with a shiny badge that reflected light each time he moved said, "Let's go ma'am, take your children somewhere else. He won't follow you".

She closed the door, and we drove away.

Life was changing, it's amazing what children learn and remember. At the time I wasn't able to comprehend what was going on with my family, but I knew something was different.

A few weeks had passed, and life was back to the "normal" I once knew. My parents were back together, we were back in our house, and it appeared that nothing had ever been wrong. There were no more police officers and no more yelling. With every passing day, the memory of that incident faded further into the back of my mind.

*** 

"Mr. Juarez…"

I heard in a faint voice.

"Mr. Juarez?" Principal Garcia repeated himself, as I snapped into focus.

"I'm sorry sir. What did you say?" I asked, feeling a bit embarrassed.

"I was asking if you're ready to head inside the classroom. The students have already been told you're coming in. Is everything okay?" he asked, concerned.

"Yes sir, I'm ready. My apologies, I was lost in my thoughts."

He opened the door for us. While he and Allen made their way to the back of the room, I stood in the front to introduce myself.

"Good morning everyone. My name is Roy Juarez Jr. Thank you so much for letting me join your class today. Sorry if I kept you waiting. The story I'm about to tell you is never easy. Every time I tell it, I have to relive it, and it hurts. As I stood outside the door, I was recalling a time I heard my mother being beaten in the middle of the night by my father…"

At the end of the presentation, I knew these students were hardened by their life situation. There weren't as many tears as the other schools and, I could only hope my words would help encourage them not to give up.

## Thoughts of Suicide

The tour made it back to Las Vegas, and the first thing I did was drop the car off to get the trunk fixed. We were lucky enough that my mentor let us borrow her car to get around. Our first presentation was at Rancho High School in North Las Vegas.

When we arrived, I was nervous we wouldn't have an audience. I was told that they didn't make the assembly mandatory but left it up to the teachers to decide whether or not they would bring their class to the assembly. The school counselor assured me that to entice the teachers, a link was sent out with my website and video. To my astonishment, I was told over 2,400 students and teachers showed up. A surge of excitement came over my body. I reminded Allen to make sure to take some pictures because up until that point, this was my largest audience on tour. I poured my heart and soul into the presentation.

At the end, I began taking questions from the audience when one young lady stood up, with tears in her eyes. She was towards the back of the auditorium, but I could clearly see her pigtails and the light pink dress she wore. With a crack in her voice, she asked, "When you were homeless, and it was hard, did you ever think about suicide?"

I was taken aback, not knowing how to react. I looked at the other students in the room who had their lips shut, breathing cautiously through their noses. I caught the eye of a teacher who showed the same concern I was feeling. This girl wasn't just asking a question, she was reaching deep into herself.

As she stood there crying, I was searching for my own composure. I dug deep into my past, looking for the right thing to say, the right situation to share. I knew what I needed to share with her.

I asked, "May I share a story with you? It's a story that's difficult to tell because it's about one of the hardest days of my life." I didn't want to share the story, but I hoped it would help her. I decided to put it in the book as well, with the hope that it will help others too.

The audience was quiet, but a more profound silence fell over the auditorium. I believe the young lady's classmates were able to see the pain she was in. She nodded her head, letting me know it was okay to share my story. Immediately, my voice cracked as I shared:

Once, this family took me in, and I noticed things were going much better than usual. Honestly, better than I had ever imagined. Even though I had been let down so many times, asked to leave so many homes, I honestly felt this family loved me. While I was living there, I had the chance to go back to school and began making friends. Everyone at school was excited because there was going to be a school dance and I really wanted to go. All my friends were going; it was going to be great. I asked my new family for permission to go to the dance, and without hesitation, the lady of the house, Mrs. Mitchell, said, "Of course."

I was so excited she gave me the money to buy my ticket. The next day at school, I told my friends that I was going! As the days passed by I was trying to figure out what to wear. I didn't have any name brand clothes in my bag, but it didn't matter. I took out my one button up shirt and my newest looking jeans. I made sure that I washed and ironed them. I wanted to look my best.

When I got home from school, the first thing I did was remind Mrs. Mitchell it was the day of the dance. She was so kind and seemed genuinely excited for me. I was even asked, "What are you going to wear?" I ran to the closet where I hung up my ironed clothes and proudly showed off my jeans and creased shirt. As the evening approached, I started to get ready for the dance. I pulled out my bag, which I considered my home, and I started to repack everything I owned. I never left home without it. I had learned from past experiences that I never knew if I would be allowed back.

I refolded my clothes, placed my dirty clothes in plastic bags to keep my clean clothes smelling fresh, I had my notepad and pen, my New International Version Bible, a toothbrush, and toothpaste. It was just about time to go when I approached her and asked, "It's almost time for the dance, will you please take me?" I stood proudly in front of her, dressed up with my bag hanging over my shoulder.

She said, "You look very nice."

With a big smile, I thanked her.

We loaded into the car and headed for the school. The closer we got, the more excited I became. I couldn't wait to see all my new friends. As we pulled up to the school, Mrs. Mitchell asked me, "You have my number, right?"

I replied, "Yes ma'am."

"Okay great. Just call me when you're ready to get picked up."

I looked at her, gave her a huge smile, I couldn't thank her enough. At that moment I felt "normal," I felt like life was getting better, it was going to be okay. I jumped out of the car and headed to the gym.

It was a great night! All my new friends were there, dressed up, and we were looking hot! Well, at least in our minds. I was excited because I knew how to dance to all the Spanish and country songs they were playing; I had learned from my sisters growing up. That's a beautiful memory I have with my sisters that I will always hold very close to my heart.

Growing up, when things were good—at least through the eyes of a kid— my parents used to have the best Christmas parties. We had a huge living room, and in one corner my Dad set up a jukebox. The rest of the living room became the dance floor. All my family would come over; all seven of my aunts and uncles and their partners. My entire family loves to dance, my uncles taught my sisters, then the movie "Urban Cowboy" took over as their teacher. My sisters would watch that movie over and over. During the dance scenes, they would press pause and learn their dance moves frame by frame. I would sit on the floor with my legs crossed and watch them. It seemed like every week they got better. Eventually, my sister said, "Roy, you need to learn to dance!" They would spend hours teaching me to two-step, cumbia, and how to spin them in the coolest ways.

I was able to use everything my sisters taught me at my school dance. It was so much fun, for a second I forgot I was homeless, and my family was scattered. But then I looked up at the large, battered clock on the gym wall. It was getting closer to the end of the dance, and I needed to call my new family. I excused myself from my friends and made my way to the front office. As I approached the office door, I could see a larger woman, with bold pink glasses, sitting inside. I slowly pushed the door open and peeked in.

The woman looked up and asked, "Hey there, can I help you?"

I let the door close behind me and said, "Hi ma'am, my name is Roy, may I please use your phone?"

"Of course!" She turned her phone around to me and instructed me, "You have to dial 9 first."

I reached into my pocket and pulled out a crumpled piece of paper where I had written Mrs. Mitchell's phone number. I dialed 9 followed by the phone number, and the phone began to ring. The phone rang and rang and rang. I was a little confused because I knew she told me to call her when I was ready to get picked up. I quickly hung up and tried the number again just in case I dialed it wrong. The phone rang and rang and rang. I hung up the phone, and this wave of fear came over me. *What if she wasn't coming back?*

I turned to the lady in the office and said, "Ma'am can I just come back in a few minutes and use your phone?"

She nodded and gave me a warm smile.

I smiled back, but I wasn't feeling any warmth inside.

When I got back to my friends in the gym, I pretended everything was okay. I didn't want them to know that I was scared, scared that Mrs. Mitchell wasn't coming back, and I would be on the streets again. About 15 minutes later, I excused myself from my friends once more and made my way back to the office. I was greeted with the same warm smile as I walked in the door.

I pointed to the phone sitting on the table, "Hey, I'm back, may I please use your phone again?"

"Of course," she replied as she turned the phone around.

I reached back in my pocket and pulled the phone number out once again. I pressed 9 and dialed out, making sure I pushed each number correctly. The phone began to ring; it rang and rang and rang. With each ring, my heart sunk deeper and my face drooped. I hung up the phone and instead of leaving I sat down in the front office. The office lady looked at me and asked if everything was okay.

I responded with a lie, "Yes ma'am, everything is fine. If my mom doesn't answer, I'll call my grandma to pick me up."

Little did she know I wasn't calling my mom or my grandmother. So much was going through my heart and mind! I caught myself just staring at the phone. Deep down I hoped she saw the missed calls on her caller ID and would call back, but the phone never rang. After about 5 minutes, a long 5 minutes, I asked, "Ma'am, can I call my grandma?"

"Yes Roy, go right ahead."

This time I didn't have to reach into my pocket, I had the number clinched in my hand, the paper was evidence of my fear; it was wet from the sweat on my palms. I un-crumbled the small piece of paper and carefully dialed the number one last time. The phone rang and rang and rang.

I felt panicked, so I said, "Hi… um, grandma… it's me, Roy… My mom isn't picking up her phone; will you please come get me from the school?" I paused for a brief second, nodded my head and mumbled, "mhmm," as if I was agreeing with her on the other end. Then I continued, "Okay, I'll wait for you outside. Thank you, grandma." I was hoping the office lady couldn't hear the phone ringing on the other end as I spoke over it.

I hung up and tried looking at her with a fake sense of relief, "I finally got an answer! My grandma is coming."

"That's good to hear," and gave me that warm smile again.

I smiled back hoping she wouldn't see my pain. I grabbed my bag, "Bye Miss."

"Goodbye Roy, have a good night!"

Oh, how I wished it was going to be a good night. I walked out the front of the school and passed by other kids getting picked up by their parents. I could hear the ones that were waiting; they were laughing and still enjoying the night. I didn't want any of my new friends to see me, so I ran to the side of the school. How I wished this would have been my new school, my new life.

The night was cold, and I walked for what seemed like miles. I must have wiped my tears every other step. My 15-year-old heart and mind couldn't understand what was happening and I just wanted to know, why? What was so wrong with me? What did I do so wrong that nobody wanted me? Beyond that, why did she have to lie to me? She could have just told me that my time with her family was up and I would have understood, I was used to it. Anything seemed better than being dumped at a school dance. Why give me hope and tell me, "Call me when you're ready to get picked up." My heart was so broken.

As I walked, the night grew darker, and I was scared. I didn't know where I was going to go. Who would I call? As I walked, I came to a bridge that was over a creek. I stopped midway across. That's when it all hit me. I could no longer contain my emotions. I stood there staring over the bridge, about 35 yards over the water. My tears fell from my face into the darkness below and in that moment, I said to myself, "Jump. Just do it, Roy. Nobody wants you anyway. Your mom doesn't want you, your dad hates you, your grandparents don't want you. Your aunts and uncles don't want you. Jump!"

I stood there and cried and cried and cried. I thought I was going to do it. I wanted to. I was nothing but a burden to everyone.

I paused from my story, still looking into the audience, tears falling from my face in front of hundreds of students. I wiped my eyes with the fingers of my right hand. As I scanned the crowd, I could see so many tears on their faces as well. Everyone was a blur, except that one young girl who asked the question. I focused my attention into the eyes of that precious young girl and told her, "Mija, I'm so glad I didn't jump that night. If I had jumped, I would have never lived to see how beautiful life can be. I would have never lived to see my little sister and brother grow up, I would have never met my nieces, I would have never lived to see my mother happy again. Mija, we can't give up. Life gets better, but you have to be here to see it. You can't check out early."

She stood there in tears as her friend next to her stood up to comfort her.

At the end of the assembly, I asked her to please stay and speak with me. I knew that I had to get in my car and keep driving, but not before I left her in the right hands. After every student left, we sat there and talked, the counselor at the school sat near her and assured her she was going to be okay. They were going to be there for her. We embraced and wished each other well.

I walked to the car where Allen had been waiting for me.

He said, "How is that girl? I didn't want to hang around afterwards because I wanted her to be able to open up to y'all."

"Thanks man, she's hurting but in good hands," I mumbled.

As we drove away from the school I sat in silence, wiping the tears from my face.

# CHAPTER EIGHT

## If You Want to Leave, That's Fine

WHILE DRIVING, I received a call from an unknown number but recognized the Phoenix area code, and that's where Allen and I were headed the next morning.

"Hello, this is Roy Juarez Jr.," I answered.

"Roy? As in the speaker Roy Juarez Jr.? Homeless-by-Choice Roy?" a friendly and

soft-spoken voice asked on the other end.

"Yes ma'am. This is Roy Juarez Jr. speaking," I chuckled.

"Oh wow! I didn't think you'd actually answer your own phone," the woman laughed. "I'm Dolores Martinez. I'm calling from Carl Hayden High School; do you have a moment to talk?"

"Hi Dolores. Yes, now is a good time. How can I help you?"

"Our principal sent out an email last week that you were coming to speak at our campus and needed somewhere to stay. I was impressed by your website; my husband Michael and I would love to host you!"

"Mrs. Martinez, thank you very much for the offer. I'd love to stay with you all, but I must let you know that I'm not traveling alone. I have my assistant, Allen, traveling with me."

"Oh, that isn't a problem, we can make room for Allen too."

"Thank you so much, we really appreciate and, I forgot to say, yes ma'am, I do answer my own phone," I laughed.

She chuckled, "Of course, we'd be happy to host you! We think what you're doing is so amazing. When are you planning to arrive in Phoenix?"

"We'll be in town by tomorrow evening," I answered.

"Okay great. If you'd like, I can make you both dinner."

"That'd be awesome! We love a home cooked meal!"

"Perfect. Now you have my number, feel free to call or text me if anything comes up on the drive here."

"Thank you Mrs. Martinez, we'll see you soon, I look forward to meeting Michael and you," I said before hanging up the phone.

I looked over at Allen, "Hey, now we have a place to stay in Phoenix. She seemed nice."

He looked back at me with tired eyes and replied, "Well, at least we won't have to sleep in the car."

The next afternoon Allen and I headed for Phoenix. The drive to the Martinez household wasn't long. We arrived just before nightfall and spent the evening getting acquainted. It felt like one of my family gatherings, everyone was loud and chatty. The three boys at dinner were super excited (the oldest of the four who still lived at home, Chris, stayed in his room) to have a guest in their home. The whole Martinez family were like old friends, we constantly laughed with each other. For dinner, we had Dolores' famous green chili! While she was cooking, the aromas of the roasting tomatoes, garlic, and salsa verde were mouthwatering. To this day, every time I'm in Phoenix, that's what I crave!

The next morning, as we all got ready to head to the high school, Dolores pulled me aside. She pulled down her wire-framed glasses and brushed her brown bangs from her forehead before she began.

"Roy, I wanted to ask, could you avoid mentioning that you're staying with us when you give your presentation? Since my son, Chris, goes to the school, he doesn't really want any of his friends to know we're hosting you. You know he's young, so I guess he's a little embarrassed."

I could tell she was uncomfortable with her request, but it didn't bother me.

"Of course, it's not a problem. I'll be sure not to mention it. I don't want his friends to think he's lame," I winked.

She let out a sigh of relief, "Thank you for being so understanding."

Once we arrived at the school, Dolores introduced us to Principal Ybarra. He was a delightful man whose smile peaked through his Yosemite Sam mustache. As we walked into his office, it was decorated with his students' accolades. He made sure to point several of them out to me and described each of them with pride.

Principal Ybarra and I reviewed the headcount, which was important to me because then I could calculate the total number of students we had reached on tour. When it was finally time, we made our way to the auditorium.

The students started to file in when I saw Chris. It wasn't hard to spot him because he towered over the students around him. I almost waved, forgetting he didn't want anyone to know his family was hosting me. I casually put my arm back down and laughed to myself as I greeted the other students. I saw him walk to the very back of the auditorium and thought, *Wow, he really didn't want anyone to know we knew each other.* I enjoyed being at the entrance as students arrived, so I could see all of their faces. When the last of them trickled in, I quickly made it back to the stage as they filled in the empty seats.

While Principal Ybarra was introducing me, he warned the students to be on their best behavior. I looked out into the audience and there were so many students. I was told that there would be over 1,100 in each of my two presentations that day.

Halfway through my story, a young man stood up from his seat and started making his way towards the aisle. This wasn't unusual for me. Sometimes, when I was speaking, students would have to leave because my story had triggered something within them. What he did next is what made the presentation memorable. The young man didn't follow the aisle to the exit but instead continued straight down towards the stage. At first, I wondered, *did I say something to offend him? Was he about to charge at me?* As he got closer, it appeared as though he was crying.

His classmates stared at him and began to whisper to each other, wondering what he was doing. The young man pretended not to notice as he walked up the stairs on the side of the stage and continued towards me. I finally paused because I wasn't sure what he was doing either. When he finally reached me, he opened his arms and wrapped them around me.

"I just felt like I needed to give you a hug sir," he said with a tear-stained face.

I put my arms around him. At that moment I thought, *What is this kid going through that he's willing to come up on stage, and let his peers see his brokenness?* As quickly as he came on stage, he was walking back to his seat, wiping his tears.

I continued my presentation by saying, "Mijo, thank you for being so brave, I needed that hug. Can we all give him a round of applause?"

The students, even those who were just whispering, stood up and clapped for the young man as he made his way back to his seat. A couple of his classmates even gave him a high five!

At the end of the assembly, I closed with a question and answer session. I was asked most of the usual questions; what happened to Baby Ray? Are you still close to your family? How did you learn to forgive your mom?

During one of my replies, I heard a student yell out from the very back of the auditorium. I looked closer and could see it was someone sitting near Chris.

"I'm sorry mijo, I can't hear you. Can you speak louder?" I asked.

"Can I give you something?" He yelled.

"Well, is it gonna hurt?" I asked, laughing.

The audience laughed with me, but the student ignored my comment and started running to the stage. He didn't bother using the steps, but instead jumped on the stage and handed me a bag of Hot Cheetos. A little surprised, I looked down at the bag then watched him run back as the other students cheered.

"Thank you mijo," I said into the mic I was holding, "I'll be sure to snack on these when I'm on the road."

After the assembly, the young man who came on stage to hug me sat in the auditorium waiting for everyone to leave. When the last student walked out, he got up and walked towards me. I looked at him and said, "Mijo, that was a brave thing you did. Is everything okay?" For the next 15 minutes, he poured his heart out.

Principal Ybarra and Allen stood patiently by the entrance, waiting for the young man to finish. Once we were done, we both walked towards the exit. Principal Ybarra put his hand on the student's shoulder and asked, "You okay? How about you stop by my office during lunch." The student agreed and headed for class.

As we walked towards the front of the school, Principal Ybarra said, "Wow, that was amazing. I have never had my students so quiet." He got even more animated when he continued, "Hot Cheetos are like gold around here. The fact that he gave you them says a lot."

Once we made it to the front door, I thanked him for allowing us to come and said, "We'll see you after lunch for the second presentation."

It's a great feeling to know that I was able to connect with the audience. To make matters even better, later that night, Dolores informed me that Chris had told all his friends he was hosting me. I guess I wasn't so lame after all. I love that kid and I'm thankful we are still great friends today.

It isn't only the students who are able to connect with my message, but also the adults who are in the room to hear me speak. They may not as quick to come up to me and share their story the way the students do but expressing the importance of my message through word of mouth means just as much to me. For example, after the presentation at Chris' high school, I ended up speaking 17 times in 5 days, all because of word of mouth. This was crazy because when we arrived in Phoenix, I only had 4 presentations lined up!

At one of my presentations, Allen and I were invited to a legislative dinner. We thought this would be a great opportunity to network, so we gladly accepted the invitation. It was at an upscale restaurant, Rustler's Rooste, so we made sure to clean up nicely.

As we were at dinner, conversing with other guests, one woman was a bit chattier than the others, perhaps it was the glass of wine she had. We had been speaking to her for quite a while, when she turned to Allen and said, "I don't mean to be too forward, but I really think you should meet my daughter. You'd be good for her."

"Oh… Okay," he said, shrugging his shoulders.

The woman pulled out her phone and showed him a picture.

To our surprise, she said, "Let me give you her number so you can text her."

We went about the rest of our night, joking about what had happened. It wasn't until the next day that Allen decided to reach out, not thinking that she would reply, but she did! They texted back and forth for a couple of days, and by day three they were calling each other "Edward and Bella," lovers from the recently released movie, Twilight. I couldn't believe it. Yuck!

We were only supposed to be in town for a week, so by the fifth day of our stay with the Martinez family, I jokingly asked Allen, "Hey man, when are you gonna break it to her that you're leaving town to cross the country?"

He turned around and looked at me with a serious expression, "About that..." he said.

I laid on the bed in Chris' room, listening to what he was going to say, but he suddenly stopped. I looked up from my phone.

"About what? You need help telling her or something? Cause I can tell her for you if you want," I teased.

"Naw Roy, it's not that."

I sat up on the bed.

"Okay, then what is it? What's the problem?"

Allen put his hands in his pockets and scrunched his shoulders together.

"Roy... I don't think I'm leaving with you. I'm staying here, in Phoenix, with Bella..."

My mouth shot open. I tried to break the tension with a laugh and asked, "You're joking right?"

"Naw man, I'm not. Look, Roy. I'm sorry. I know it sounds crazy, but I'm staying in Phoenix..." he repeated himself.

I wish I could tell you the backstory to this, but I promised Allen I wouldn't repeat it... but if you take me out for coffee, I just might spill the beans. Haha!

I threw my hands in the air and just as I was about to yell from frustration, I got off the bed and walked out of the room. How could one of my good friends leave the tour for a girl he only knew for five days, in a city he was unfamiliar with?! They had only been on one date. I cooled off in the living room for a couple of minutes then went back to Chris' room.

"Allen, if you wanna stay, that's fine, but I have a tour to do. You know I'm leaving in a couple of days and honestly man, if you're gonna stay here in town you might as well start getting your stuff to her place now," I said pointing to his belongings that were scattered across the room.

He was already packing up most of his things. Understanding how upset I was, Allen replied, "Alright Roy, that's fine." He paused for a short moment, then said, "I just need to get the rest of my stuff from your trunk... Bella's already waiting outside."

"Outside?!"

As if the situation couldn't get any worse.

With his head down, he replied, "Yeah... I had told her we were supposed to leave today, and I needed to tell you. She's been waiting for me outside."

"Well then, let's go get your things from my trunk," I snarked.

We walked out to the car. I was still in disbelief, but Allen's new girlfriend was waiting at the end of the driveway with her trunk opened. He pulled out the suitcase and walked it over to her car. Just as he was about to place it in her trunk, I stopped him.

"Hey man, that's my luggage you got there," I said unsympathetically.

The luggage really didn't matter to me, but I was being bitter. I shouldn't have, but I was. Allen looked at me, holding eye contact as he unzipped the bag, and dumped everything out into her trunk.

"Thanks," I said, smiling in his face, "I can get you a plastic bag instead if you want."

He rolled his eyes at me as I turned around to go back inside.

I helped him get together the rest of what he had brought and wished him good luck before he left. It had only been 2 weeks into the tour, and I had already lost my traveling assistant.

As the week came to an end, I became even closer to Michael, Dolores and the rest of the Martinez family. They welcomed me with open arms from the beginning, and I felt I could talk to them about anything. Michael reminded me a lot of my siblings, he loved to joke and tease me. Being a larger man, with a dark black goatee, he looked intimidating but Michael has the heart of a saint.

The day before leaving, Michael, Dolores and I were having lunch, I explained to them the real reason why I thought Allen had abandoned the tour.

"Guys, honestly I don't really blame Allen for leaving the tour. I'm under so much stress I probably wouldn't want to be around me either. I didn't think it would affect the tour, but yesterday I had to cancel my presentations in Tucson. It wasn't only his company I enjoyed, but it was nice to have someone drive to the next city or help me contact schools. I need to work on how I let stress affect me. I need to be better and not bitter," I vented to them.

Michael said, "Roy, I'm sure the tour is tough, but you're doing a great thing. Allen is a good guy, but you are too. Don't be so hard on yourself."

"Thanks, but I don't know how I'll do this alone. It's been so hard and now to do it by myself. I don't know if I have it in me."

Michael looked at me, rubbing his chin. I could tell he was trying to help me come up with a solution when he finally said, "Roy, why don't you take our daughter Val with you?"

Mrs. Martinez stopped mid-bite and looked at her husband with wide eyes. She gulped down her food, and to my surprise, she said, "That's a great idea Michael! It would be good for her! Take her with you Roy, I'm sure she'll enjoy it."

I was stunned, and jokingly said, "I'm not into child trafficking!"

They started laughing, and Michael said, "She's twenty-one, I think this would be an amazing opportunity for her to experience life and learn more about herself."

Dolores reached into her purse, pulled out her phone and continued her thought, "Actually, I'll call her right now to see what she thinks."

"No! Not right now Dolores, she's at work. We'll bring it up to her tonight at dinner, like an intervention," Michael laughed.

Sure enough, later that night, Val showed up to the house for dinner. She was dressed stylishly, with a deep purple blouse and fitted jeans, as though we were going out to eat. Her silky long black hair curled down just below her shoulders, and her full cheeks had a natural glow. During dinner, Dolores brought the idea up to Val. I sat at the table nervous about what she might think. We had only met once before because she had her own apartment.

"Val, we invited you to dinner tonight because we wa—"

"Want to have an intervention," Michael interrupted.

"Shut up Michael!" she said laughing.

Then she continued, "Val, we invited you to dinner tonight because we want you to consider going with on tour with Roy. Your dad and I think it would be a great experience for you. You'd be traveling, and it'd be a great way to learn more about yourself and see what's out there."

Val raised her eyebrows, wrinkling her forehead. Her eyes bounced back and forth between her parents.

We all leaned forward towards Val, anxious about how she would respond.

I was shocked when she threw caution to the wind and agreed to quit her job the next day, so she could join me on tour. That night she went home to pack up, and in less than 24 hours, we were on the road. I was relieved to have someone on tour with me to help out.

Val and I picked up as though we had known each other for years! We were kindred spirits with a similar sense of humor. She was a tremendous help, but I could tell that living on the road was starting to weigh on her. She began talking about missing her family and friends, or what she would be doing if she was home. I was aware the tour was a lot of work for a little money, so I knew I was asking a lot of Val.

Finally, after a few weeks of nonstop work, Val and I had a week's worth of downtime. We decided to take my mentor up on an offer she made to fly us to Vegas and spend the week with her as a way to recharge. This meant I could actually go back home to Nick's house for a week! I could also hang out with my best friend Goy and spend time with my mentor, *How could I say no?*

This would also help us save on meals and relieve us from the perils of trying to find a place to sleep. The Martinez family was excited to hear that we would be so close to them, they decided to meet us in Vegas to visit Val. After a few days in Vegas, Val confessed that she hated the living arrangement and I couldn't blame her. I knew it was horrible on the road, sleeping in unfamiliar places, irregular driving hours, and me for company!

"I wish I could say it gets better but honestly, it doesn't," I said.

"I mean, you're used to this, aren't you? After being on tour for a while, aren't you used to unfamiliarity?" Val asked.

She had a point, but I knew her question was rhetorical and there was no getting used to this life. I stayed quiet and waited for her to finish her thought.

"I just can't live on the road anymore Roy. It was an impulsive decision on my part. I was even asking Goy for some advice the other night. I didn't know how to tell you what I was feeling. When we were talking he offered up his spare bedroom to me if I chose to stay here instead of going back on tou—"

"Wait, he what?" I interrupted.

"Goy said if I wanted to I could stay here instead of going back to Texas with you," she said cautiously. "I took him up on his offer, so when you leave, I'm gonna stay here for a bit before I go back home."

"Okay mija, that's fine. Thank you for telling me, and I'm glad you were able to experience what life on the road was like. I hope you were able to learn a couple of things this past month," I said trying to hide my frustration, not with her, but with my situation.

I had seen it coming but couldn't be upset with her. Val and I didn't know each other outside of the week her family had hosted me. She took a chance by coming out on tour with me, and I could respect her for that. Truthfully, I was just frustrated because once again I was put in a situation where I needed to find another traveling assistant.

# CHAPTER NINE

## Don't Give Them Your Future

### Sweetwater, Texas - 3 Months into the Tour

THE SUN WAS setting, and I had been driving for hours. With each mile, my eyelids got heavier. I had to force myself to keep them open. Despite my exhaustion, excitement rushed through my body. I was finally about to see my family and be in a familiar place again. Living on the road for three months, I hadn't stayed anywhere long enough for it to become "familiar." I was sleeping on strangers' couches, in my car, and occasionally a hotel bed, so to stay in my sister Tammy's guest bedroom sounded like heaven. No matter how tired I was, I was determined not to stop driving until I reached San Antonio and arrived at her house.

At that time, my sister didn't live in the best neighborhood, so when I arrived, I made sure to take everything out of the car, just in case. I must have been sleepwalking because I don't even remember the conversation I had with my sister that evening. I just remember my sister waking me up the next morning and hearing her say, "Roy I think someone broke into your car!"

I was still in a daze, "What are you talking about?"

She asked, "Did you have a stereo?"

Her words finally clicked, and I snapped, "Are you serious?!"

I jumped out of bed and walked outside. Sure enough, the one thing I forgot to take down was the faceplate of my car stereo. Now, the entire system was gone.

I felt furious but also hurt. I know this sounds crazy, but I loved my stereo. I had just bought it, had it installed, and it was my only companion on the long drives from city to city, since I no longer had anyone traveling with me. It came with a microphone, so I could make calls while driving which was convenient. If I wasn't listening to music, I was talking with schools trying to set up my next speaking engagement. In the evenings, I was on the phone with friends who were trying to keep me from falling asleep. If I had only remembered to take the faceplate down with me the night before... but I was so tired, I hadn't even thought of it. I stood there staring at the broken lock on my car door and the wires that were hanging out from where my stereo should have been.

All I could think was, *Are you kidding me?* The tour was already low on funds from lack of donations. Now, I would have to replace the lock and eventually wait until I got enough money to replace the stereo. Honestly, I wanted to cry out of frustration and stress. I turned to my sister who was still standing next to me with her hand on her hip, slowly shaking her head from side to side. With a wry smirk, she said,

"I told you Roy, screw these people. Why are you trying to help them? None of them care about you. No one wants to donate to the tour, screw them all!"

I turned to acknowledge my sister, her long black hair was pulled back in a hairclip. I dropped my head back, looking towards the sky, trying to figure out what I was going to do next.

I said, "This pisses me off so much. Here I am trying to help people, and someone comes along and does this! But I can't give up. This just proves there is so much work to be done."

"Whatever, I told you, people suck. You do too much for them," My sister said as she walked off.

I knew Tammy was only speaking from a place of love for me, but did she have a point? I had to remind myself, *Better, never bitter.* I hesitated as my attention focused on the damage again. I continued, *It's okay, it's only stuff.*

*This just goes to show how much work I have to do. I need to reach more young people. Everything happens for a reason. I'm not sure what the reason is, but they probably needed it more than I did… it's okay.*

Don't get me wrong, I was extremely agitated, but I couldn't allow it to paralyze me mentally or emotionally. I went back into the house and started getting ready for church. My entire family knew I was coming into town and we planned to meet at the church where my adopted parents were pastors. This made it easy for me to see a lot of my family because my biological mom, grandmother, aunts, and several of my cousins attended Offerings of Peace Church.

I was now running late, due to the whole car situation. I got dressed as quickly as I could because I knew my adopted dad would be waiting for me. He wouldn't want me to be late, for him "on time" was 15 minutes early. I kept rushing to get ready and tried keeping my mind off the fact that someone had just broken into my car. I guess it was a good thing I was heading to church!

I ran out the front door and jumped into my car. As I left Tammy's house, I didn't realize I was headed the wrong way. My sister had just moved, and I was unfamiliar with the neighborhood. As I drove down the street, I noticed an elderly woman pushing herself in a wheelchair. It had just rained the night before, so I made sure to pass by her slowly because I didn't want to splash her with the huge puddle at the side of the road. I glanced over to see this fragile, grandmotherly woman. I continued to the stop sign, but I couldn't help to look in my rearview mirror as I watched her struggle to make her way.

As I sat there, I thought, *Roy, go back and help her. How dare you just pass her by. How many people saw you in need when you were a teenager and didn't help you?* I put my car in park, got out, and started walking down the street towards her. I didn't want to scare her, so from a distance, I yelled, "Hi ma'am, are you okay? Are you trying to get somewhere?" What I didn't realize was that she mostly spoke Spanish but, even though I wasn't fluent, I knew enough to understand her. She scattered her native tongue with English.

As I got closer, she said, "Voy a H.E.B.," which was the local grocery store. There was no way she was going to make it wheeling herself around. The nearest H.E.B. was at least a mile away, and she would have had to cross a major highway.

"Ma'am, I am headed that way, I don't mind driving you to the store."

With a big smile, and in her broken English she said, "Gracias, that be fine."

I wanted to make her feel as comfortable as possible and not feel intimidated by me even though I was dressed in my Sunday best.

I said, "I'm Roy, it's very nice to meet you."

She smiled, "I'm Mrs. Sanchez."

I wheeled her over to my car, helped her in, and placed the wheelchair in my trunk. During the ride, I tried to keep Mrs. Sanchez talking, so there wasn't any awkward silence between us. I can still remember all the words I butchered.

As soon as we got to the store, I pulled up to the very front and began helping Mrs. Sanchez out of my car and into the wheelchair. It was awkward for me because I didn't know exactly how to transfer her with ease. I noticed a store employee walking by and called out to her, "Excuse me ma'am."

The young lady walked over to me and asked, "Yes sir, how can I help you?"

I wasn't sure what to say, but tried to explain, "This woman, Mrs. Sanchez, is probably going to need help with her shopping. I don't know her, I just gave her a ride."

She seemed confused but said, "Oh, okay…" as she glanced down at Mrs. Sanchez who was still adjusting in her wheelchair.

I looked down at her as well and said, "Okay ma'am, it was great meeting you. This nice young lady will help you from here." I smiled goodbye, quickly ran around my car, and jumped into the driver's seat because I was already late for church. I could picture my adopted dad waiting for me, wondering why I wasn't "on time."

I put the car into drive and was about to take off when the store employee knocked on my passenger window. I rolled down the window and asked, "Yes ma'am, is everything okay?"

She looked at me with slight concern then said, "This lady would like to know how she is going to get home when she's done shopping."

Oh my goodness! I hadn't even considered it. I figured I would just drop her off, and my good deed was done, but it was a valid question. I couldn't think of an answer quick enough, "Uhh, give me one second ma'am, let me park."

I drove down one of the isles and took the first open parking spot. I walked over to Mrs. Sanchez and the store employee.

"Thank you ma'am, I'll help her from here," I got behind the wheelchair and pushed her into the grocery store. Luckily Mrs. Sanchez didn't have a long list of items, nor were they perishable. We were in and out within 10 minutes of arriving. That was in part due to how fast I was pushing her wheelchair! After helping Mrs. Sanchez into the car and putting her wheelchair back into my trunk, I panicked over how upset my adopted dad was going to be about my lateness.

When I got back into the driver seat, I looked at Mrs. Sanchez and explained, "Mrs. Sanchez, before I picked you up I was headed to meet my parents. I'm running really late. My parents are ministers, and I'm meeting them at their church. Will you come with me?" I had no clue if she understood a word I had said, but I didn't know how to translate all that into Spanish.

Mrs. Sanchez nodded, and just said, "Okay."

A sense of relief came over me. However, it didn't last that long because as we made our way to the church, I glanced over at Mrs. Sanchez, and I noticed she was crying. I got scared. Did she not understand what I was trying to explain to her about being late to church? I didn't want her to think I was kidnapping her or something. What if she misunderstood me due to the language barrier?

I asked, "Mrs. Sanchez, are you okay?"

Still crying, she said, "I don't know what to do."

Confused, I said slowly, "I don't understand. You said you didn't mind coming with me. I know I'm in a rush, but if you're not comfortable, I can take you home. It's not a big deal, I promise."

"I don't know what to do. Yo no soy de este country, I just lost mi house,

I cannot pay. My oldest son no habla conmigo porque his girlfriend no like me y mi ortro hijo es adicto to drogas. I don't know what I going to do."

She wiped the tears from her eyes.

I had no clue what to say. I had no way of helping this lady, I mean, I was on a tour that didn't have any sponsors, and I was living off the generosity of the communities I served. I knew I had to say something because the silence was so awkward. "Mrs. Sanchez, I don't even live here, but maybe my parents could help."

She didn't even look at me but instead stared out the window. We drove the rest of the way in silence.

As we arrived, my adopted dad was standing outside the church. I knew he was waiting for me because the service had already started. When he saw my car pulling in, I could see the smile on his face. I parked near the ramp entrance to make it easy to get Mrs. Sanchez into the building. My adopted dad greeted me from the door, "You made it, I started to think you weren't gonna come." I then noticed his puzzled face while I was pulling the wheelchair out of my trunk. I laughed to myself and continued to help Mrs. Sanchez into her chair and pushed her up the ramp. My adopted dad held the door open for us as we entered.

As I walked by him, I whispered, "I'll explain in a minute."

I escorted Mrs. Sanchez into the main sanctuary and positioned her wheelchair in the back of the room. I didn't want to cause a ruckus since the service had already started. I whispered to her, "I'll be right back." I made my way out to the foyer where my adopted dad was waiting for me.

I gave him a proper greeting.

He asked cautiously, "So… How are you?"

I laughed, "Well, it's been quite a morning…" I then explained to him about my car and how I met Mrs. Sanchez. I said, "Pastor Johnny" (which is how I refer to my adopted dad), "She really needs our help." I shared with him Mrs. Sanchez' situation and asked, "Is there anything we can do?" He suggested picking up a donation at the end of the service, which I thought was a great idea.

At the end of the service, my adopted dad went before the congregation and said, "It's come to my attention that there is a woman in need this morning. We will be passing the offering plate around and, if you find it in your heart to help, it would be greatly appreciated." The ushers passed the offering plate up and down the aisles, and a huge donation was collected. We didn't have a desire to know how much it was, so we just put it into a large Ziploc bag and handed it to Mrs. Sanchez.

After visiting with my family over a meal the church had provided, I began to drive Mrs. Sanchez home. On the way there, I glanced over and noticed she was crying again. I asked her with genuine concern, "Mrs. Sanchez, are you okay?"

She looked at me, and with caution, asked, "If mi hijo is home, you talk to him? Por favor."

"I'd love to speak with your son," I said. Although I wasn't too sure what she wanted me to say. How would I even approach the guy?

"Pero listen, you need know, I was not there para mi hijo," she continued.

"It's okay Mrs. Sanchez, we all make mistakes."

"No! I was NOT there," she repeated.

I stayed quiet and thought about how much I understood what it was like to have a mother who was absent. The silence continued, and we drove the rest of the way without saying a word.

As I parked right in front of the door to her house, the first things I noticed were the unmanicured lawn, the broken and uneven sidewalk leading to the front door, and two steps leading into the house. I thought, *How in the world has she been getting into her own house?* I helped her down the sidewalk and pulled the wheelchair up the steps and into her living room.

She said, "Wait. I check if he's home."

I have to admit, I was a bit nervous because all I knew about her son was that he was a druggie. Coming from the streets, I knew I had to be ready for anything. I quickly evaluated my environment, looked for something that could be a weapon or objects that might be in the way of me running back to my car. It may sound crazy, but you never know. I made sure to stand in the doorway with one foot in the lady's house and the other foot outside.

Mrs. Sanchez began pushing herself down the hallway and yelling. "Jose!

Jose!" and before I knew it, this young man turned the corner. He was shirtless and covered in tattoos, from his torso all the way up to his face. My heart raced.

I didn't want to show him I was anxious, so I looked at him and casually said, "Hey, what's up man?"

"What's up?" he replied. He looked at me confused, clearly wondering what the hell I was doing in his house.

"Not much man, just bringing your mom home."

"Alright, well thanks for taking care of my mom," he said as he turned around. I could tell he wanted nothing to do with me or the conversation.

"Yeah, it's no problem," I said quickly, hoping he'd turn back to me, "I took her to the grocery store, then we went to chur—"

"No, talk to him about the drug!" Mrs. Sanchez interrupted.

If I hadn't gotten his full attention, I know I had it now. At that moment my heart sank into my gut. "Uh. Man, what you do with your life is your business but let me share with you what I do. I'm on tour right now where I'm choosing to live homeless for the second time in my life," I began telling him the short summary of my life that I give when people ask me what I do for a living. I kept going, "I was homeless at 14. Eventually, my 9-year-old sister and 2-year-old brother were as well. That's when we were reunited. It was all because of domestic violence... anyway, now I've decided to live out of my car," as I pointed to it behind me, "and cross this country with the hope to inspire as many young people to never giv—"

At that moment Jose cut me off and with anger in his voice he said, "You want to know something?" He pointed at his mother. "These people were never there for me, man. As a matter of fact, my dad didn't even want me. So when I was three, he put diesel in my bottle! But guess what? It didn't kill me. And this lady? She was never there for me either." Jose took a step closer to me, looked directly into my eyes and said, with his voice further elevated, "So yeah, I break into cars to make money! What do you think about that?"

I was floored. This was more than likely the guy who broke into my car the night before. Why else would he bring up my car? I was pissed off but had to control my anger because I understood that something more important was happening here. I could always replace my lock and stereo, but I wouldn't ever get the chance to help Jose again.

Still, eyes locked, I said with more passion in my voice, "I get it, I do. I hear what you're telling me, Jose. Maybe they sucked as parents and if that is the case, let me ask you a question." He rolled his eyes as I spoke. "Hear me out man. If these people have taken so much from you already then my question is; Why are you giving them your future too?"

We stood there in silence for a brief moment until a light bulb appeared to go off in Jose's mind. He dropped his head a bit and in a more somber voice, said, "Let me tell you something, man." Jose looked up at me, eyes glossed over, "I'm out on bond. I face murder charges in two weeks."

My heart broke. Why couldn't I have met Jose earlier? Not saying I would have been able to change his situation, but at least I could have tried.

I said, "Jose, I don't even want to know if you did it. All I know is in two weeks, whichever way that coin falls, you have to stop giving your future away. Jose, we only get this life once... man, we have to make the best choices."

I stayed there a little while longer and shared with Jose that he needed to want change in his life, but the decision had to be his. However, if he wanted help, he could always call or text me. I gave Jose my number and email then made my way back to the car.

Sadly, I never heard from Jose again, and I have no idea what happened to him. I hope and pray he is living a healthier lifestyle. As activists, service providers, educators, parents, or friends, we might not get to see the impact we make in someone's life, but that shouldn't stop us from trying.

## Tammy Joins the Tour

When I was finally able to spend time with my family, we all got together at my mother's house, my sister Tammy was making her famous lasagna. They asked me about the tour, and all the new places I'd been since the last time I saw them. Inevitably, I told them about meeting the Martinez family, losing Allen, then losing Val, and how stressful it all was. They could see how exhausted I looked and urged me to end the tour.

As we all sat around the small kitchen table, my little sister Danielle said, "You've helped enough people. We love and miss you too. Come home."

"I can't mija, you don't know much these kids are hurting."

As I told more stories of the students I had met, my sister Tammy, who wasn't working at the time, offered to join me as I spoke around Texas. She couldn't guarantee that she'd be with me long, which was a great heads up, but she promised to stay as long as she could.

This was great news and perfect timing. I explained to Tammy that after my events in San Antonio, I was heading to Houston for a few weeks, but would be returning back to town because I would be speaking at the San Antonio Youth Summit. If she was serious, I could really use the help, and if it didn't work out, I could always drop her back off when I returned. She agreed to come with me and began making arrangements for her daughter, my niece, to stay with her father.

The week I was in San Antonio I had been hired by Southwest Independent School District, the district I graduated from. They were about to be my saving grace for hiring me to speak at all of their schools, from elementary to high school. Payment would be enough to get my bank accounts out of the negative, catch up on my bills, and have enough money for a couple weeks. I hoped this would be a turning point in the tour.

While Tammy was with me in Houston, the tour made no financial progress. There was virtually no money coming in because the schools I presented at weren't donating, and I was spending twice as much on food to feed my sister and I. At most, one in every five schools would contribute to the tour, but the average donation was about $100. Every day I was watching my bank account diminish. Since the tour was costing me about $8,000 a month, I couldn't afford to pay my sister and keep the tour alive.

For the third time, I knew I'd have to go at it alone. The thought of doing so frightened me, but I wasn't going to let it stop me. My sister wanted to help me, but we just couldn't get anyone to donate, and she needed to get a steady paying job to support her daughter. When we returned to San Antonio, she said, "Roy, I can continue to research and reach out to schools for you in my spare time. I wish I could travel with you, but I have to make money."

# Odessa, Texas – 5 Months into the Tour

I found myself back in West Texas for a paid speaking engagement. I was extremely excited about this event because I would be addressing the parents who were graduating from my mentors' Family Leadership Institute (FLI). A program that focuses on providing families with the knowledge, tools, and inspiration to help their children succeed in school and in life.

About a month prior I had received a call from my mentor stating her client was interested in having me speak. I jumped at the opportunity because I needed the money for the tour and I would do anything for Mrs. K. I reached out to the contact, Ms. Villaloboz, via email.

In my email, I wrote, "Dear Ms. Villaloboz, I am honored you chose me as your graduation speaker for the FLI. However, I am currently on my national Homeless by Choice tour. Would it be possible to speak at any schools or shelters while I am in town? On tour, we request an honorarium per presentation. However, if a school isn't able to provide one, I am still willing to serve. Please know that our tour does not have any grants or sponsors, and it survives off the generosity of the communities we serve. Thank you so much for your consideration."

Ms. Villaloboz loved the idea and replied, "Roy, let me see what I could do."

About a week later, I received an email from her confirming she had found several schools that were interested in being a part of the tour.

When I finally made it to Odessa, Texas, Ms. Villaloboz was kind enough to drive me to each of my events. After one of my presentations at the Family Leadership Center, I was approached by a middle-aged woman, who was well-dressed in a blue suit and had her curled hair perfectly placed. However, mascara was running down her face.

She said, "Mr. Juarez, I'm the director of a juvenile detention center. I was wondering if you would be willing to come to speak with my young men."

"I would love to, but I don't know if I have any time. From what Ms. Villaloboz has told me, my time here is fully booked. If you don't mind talking with her, maybe we can work something out," I said.

After reviewing my schedule, we were able to find some time early the following morning. I ended up waking up before my alarm; I knew it was going to be a long day, but I was ready for it. The several schools we had already visited received the message well, so I hoped this energy would keep going.

When the director of the facility, Ms. Villaloboz, and I arrived at the detention center, I was instructed it would best if I left all my personal items, including my cell phone, in the car. We walked into the building which lacked character and waited to go through the screening process.

Once it was time to be screened, I was told to empty my pockets, place what belongings I had into a tray, proceed through a metal detector and, lastly, wait to be patted down by a detention officer. The process was intimidating, but once it was complete the three of us were finally escorted through the echoing halls to where I would speak.

The room was reasonably large, with pale walls, and no windows. I was standing among a sea of white brick. I was alone because Ms. Villaloboz and the director were waiting just outside for the students. Without warning, the doors to my right and left swung open, and dozens of young men came walking in. They all looked like children and wore matching burnt-orange uniforms that looked like scrubs. Following right behind them were the officers, dressed in what looked like military attire.

As soon as the young men began sitting down, I turned to the director and asked, "Is it okay if I interact?"

She smiled at me and said, "Go ahead Roy."

I walked up to the young men and started shaking hands with whoever was willing. A few of them ignored my gesture, but it didn't faze me.

I started asking, "Hey man, what's your name?" "Where do you come from?" "Hey bro, how are you?"

There was this one young man that stood out due to his innocent childish look, as if he couldn't hurt a fly. He was of Latino descent, with not even a speck of peach fuzz on his face. You could tell he was tough but presented himself respectably, and to top it off, he had a great sense of humor. He had a conversation with me and asked just as many questions.

He asked, "Yo sir, what are you going to talk about? Are you from church or something?"

I said, "Naw mijo, I am just going to tell you a story about my life."

"That's what's up sir."

"If it's boring, just take a nap," I said jokingly.

"Naw sir, I wouldn't do that. That's rude and shit. I'm gonna listen."

"Thanks Mijo, well at least tell me what you think after."

"I got you sir."

The director stepped forward and explained to the young men why I was there. She shared that she heard me present and asked if I would come. As she handed me the floor, I prayed under my breath. "God, I know I'm not your best kid… but please give me the right words to say."

At the end of the presentation, I stood at the door saying goodbye to all the guys. Each one of them shook my hand, including the ones who ignored me before the presentation. The young man who stood out shook my hand and gave me a huge hug. I'm not sure if he was supposed to do that, but then he said, "Yo Sir, that was deep. It was nice meeting you. You should go to my old school I got cousins who need to hea—"

"Keep it moving!" yelled the guard.

Just like that, he was gone.

After I said goodbye to everyone, I walked out of the facility with the director and Ms. Villaloboz. Once outside, she started to tear up.

I asked, "Are you okay?"

She responded, "I just love my boys so much and wish life was different for them."

I knew her pain, "I can understand that. Who was that young man that you saw me talking to?"

Wiping a few tears from her eyes, she said, "That's Abel."

"Oh… Why's he in here?"

"Roy, he's in here for murder," she answered.

My jaw dropped, "Murder?"

"Yeah," she replied wiping her eyes once again. "When he was sixteen years old his father picked him up from school and told him, 'today, you're gonna kill a man.' His father was involved in all the gang violence and drug trafficking in their city, so he did it. When he went to trial, they prosecuted him as an adult."

Her eyes began to swell again. "The thing is, in about two months we have to move him to an adult facility, but we don't give him longer than two weeks to live before the rival gang kills him. He's dead, he's sixteen, and he's dead."

My heart broke hearing those words. Why didn't anyone catch Abel when he was younger? Maybe things would be different. If someone would have found him and taught him that he had a future that belonged to him—and not to his dad—then maybe, just maybe. After that, I decided crossing the country wasn't enough. There were too many kids hurting, and I had to do more to help. I wanted to reach more students and teach them that their future belongs to them, not anyone else. I then knew I had to circle the entire country and made it my personal goal to reach over 100,000 students, parents, and educators to spread my message of hope, perseverance, and the power of higher education.

## Back at the Waffle House

"How do you like those pecan waffles?" the waitress asked.

"They're delicious! Even better than I expected," I replied with a mouth full of food.

She smiled and turned over to Morgan, "What about you? Is everything tasting alright?"

"Yes, everything is great. Thank you," Morgan replied quickly, then turned back to face me. She looked at me in astonishment. "I can't believe that Roy. What happens next?"

# CHAPTER TEN

## How Sharp Was the Knife?

I WAS ALMOST done with the first six months of the tour, which I eventually called, *the first phase*. Because I decided to circle the entire country, I was going to have to raise a lot more money. Initially, I planned on keeping my room in Nick's house because I only expected to be gone for about six months, and I loved that house. However, if I was going to circle the country, I would be on the road for at least another year-and-a-half. This meant I would need to drive back to Vegas and sell as much of my stuff as possible to make money for the tour. Whatever I couldn't sell, I would store in my mentor's garage.

I had one more presentation, but luckily it was in San Antonio, Texas at George I. Sanchez Charter High School. I was going to be their 2010 graduation speaker. I was excited about the event, but to be completely honest, I was more excited to see my family. The thought of spending quality time with them sounded refreshing and rewarding. I desperately needed it after my tough journey.

Plus, it would be nice to continue working on the second phase of the tour in the comfort of my mother's home rather than some hotel or a stranger's house. While I was in town, I spent the first few days visiting family, going out to eat, and reuniting with friends. The best part was, all my siblings knew I was poor so if we went out to eat, they picked up the tab. The second half of my stay was dedicated to making phase two of the tour as successful as possible.

After a bit of planning, I wrote a post on Facebook asking if anyone was interested in joining the tour as my traveling assistant. I posted, "I'm looking for a traveling assistant on the Homeless by Choice Tour! You'll have a once in a lifetime opportunity to travel the country and help me inspire over 100,000 students. If you're interested, send me a private message, and I will provide you more detail."

Although I was reluctant to reach out, because so many people had left prematurely before, I knew I desperately needed the help.

A young man named Kenny, who liked the post, reached out to me through Facebook Messenger on several occasions. I had met Kenny briefly through mutual friends but wasn't sure if our personalities were compatible. So, I was a bit reluctant to offer him the position.

I tried to weed him out by asking him for a resume, which he eventually provided. I then asked him for a one-page essay on why he wanted to be a part of the Homeless by Choice Tour. To my surprise, he presented me with my request. While there were several grammatical errors, I was quite impressed by his persistence. I figured I'd give him a chance. I wrote Kenny back to tell him the good news.

I had an event taking place in Phoenix two weeks before I launched phase two. My offer was that I would fly him to me on a trial basis. This would be a great way to see if we were compatible. I would have him meet me in Vegas and drive with me to the conference. It would give us enough time on the road to see if we got along, which was important to me because we would be spending so much time together. After I invited him, I realized there was already a problem; I didn't know where we would stay when we returned.

I wasn't going to ask my mentor to let us both sleep on her couch since I was unacquainted with Kenny, and she had two young daughters. I felt it would be asking too much. Instead, I decided to reach out to one of my close friends, Matt, who also lived in Las Vegas and was working for my mentor at the time. My family had taken him in several times, rent-free, so I was pretty sure he would return the favor.

I dialed his number.

"Hey Roy, what's up?" he answered.

"Matt! Hey man, how you been?" I asked.

"I've been good, just working with Consuelo and trying to enjoy my free time when I can. What about you?"

"I'm doing alright, I actually just got back in town! That's why I was calling you."

"Yeah, I heard. How's the tour?" Although he asked, he sounded uninterested.

"It's been hard man, it's crazy! I knew we had issues in our country, but I never realized there are so many hurting kids out there," I paused for a moment. "I was actually calling because I've decided to extend the tour. My goal is now to circle the country and reach over 100,000 students."

"Wow, 100,000? That's a lot of kids, Roy. You think you can do it?"

I knew Matt well enough to know he was feigning his interest, but I continued to entertain the conversation.

"It'll be tough for sure, but I have to try. You know?"

"Yeah… Well, good luck with that," the uninterested tone in his voice continued. Perhaps, he didn't want to talk to me. Or did I just call him at a bad time?

"Thanks Matt. Hey, sorry if you're busy, but I was going to ask you for a favor. I have a traveling assistant coming up here next week, and we need a place to stay before the tour launches again. Do you think we can crash on your couch for two weeks? I know that's a long time, but I can give you $100 to stay and $100 for groceries. I know it's not much man, but it's all I've got," I said with a hopeful voice.

"Oh. Well, as much as I'd love to help, I can't. Sorry," he said.

Shocked that he had refused to help me, all I could think to say was, "Okay. Thanks though. Hope you have a good week."

I quickly hung up and thought about what I was going to do. I didn't want to ask my mentor, but I felt that was the only choice I had left. I dialed her number, and it rang a few times before she picked up.

"And what are you doing for your country?" she answered in a joking voice.

"I'm trying to keep a tour alive, ma'am!" I chuckled. "Which is why I am calling, I need to ask you for a huge favor. Honestly, I'm sorry I even have to ask."

"You know you can ask me anything loco, what is it?"

I swallowed hard, then asked, "Would it be possible for my new traveling assistant, Kenny, and I to stay with you for two weeks?"

"Mijo, we have the girls, and you don't really know him, do you? I saw the post you made on your Facebook. Anyone could have answered that."

"No ma'am, I've only met him once. I know it's a lot to ask, but I don't really have any more options."

My mentor stayed quiet for a brief moment. "Wait, I thought you were going to ask Matt?"

"I did ma'am. I asked him just right now, but he said no, which is why I called you."

"He said no?" She asked, surprised. "After all you've done for him?"

"Yeah, he said no. I even offered him $200 for the two weeks. I told him I'd give him $100 in groceries and $100 for letting us sleep on his couch!"

"After all you've done for him! So ungrateful. I don't know what's going on with him lately, but something's wrong. He's been calling in to work almost every Monday!" she exclaimed. "I hope he hasn't gone back to that stuff again. His excuse for calling in is always blaming it on eating a 'bad taco.' I'm going to have to talk to my husband about him. I don't need people like that in my company, people who can't look out for others."

"Oh wow, I didn't know he's been acting differently. Oh God, I hope he isn't hooked on that stuff again, too."

Changing the subject, she asked, "Do you have a place to sleep tonight mijo?"

"Yes ma'am, I'm still at Nick's house for a few more days. I'm packing up what I have left."

"Well *you're* always welcome here mijo, you know that, but let me talk to David about Kenny," she said in a loving voice.

"Yes ma'am, thank you."

"Why don't you come over to the house tomorrow for breakfast? We'll try and figure something out then."

"Thank you ma'am, I'll see to you tomorrow," I said as I hung up the phone.

I continued packing my room with Matt's response still in mind. My family had taken him in, and he quickly became a part of our family. We had helped him in so many ways.

When I was in college and Matt was still in San Antonio, I had heard through the grapevine that he was really struggling with life and abusing drugs. Because I loved this guy like a brother, I drove from Abilene to San Antonio with a plan to help him.

I called him up and said, "Hey man I'll be in San Antonio this weekend! We should hang out!"

"Hell yeah, let me know when you get into town!" Matt's voice filled with excitement.

After my Friday afternoon class, I jumped into my F150 and headed for San Antonio. As soon as I crossed the county line, I called him.

"Hey man, I just rolled into town. Where are you?"

"I am at my dad's house on the Southside."

I knew where his dad lived because I had been there many times before.

"Awesome, I'm headed in that direction, be ready for me to pick you up."

"Where are we going?" Matt asked.

I wasn't sure what to tell him. I thought I would pick him up and drive back to Abilene, but I knew it would be really late. I didn't want to give him a chance to figure out what I was doing and not come with me.

"Let's go to dinner, I'm starving! My treat," I tried to entice him.

"Your treat? Why aren't you here yet?" He laughed.

As I pulled up to his dad's house my stomach began cramping. I'm not sure if I was nervous or just hungry. As he walked towards my car I was examining him from top to bottom. I was expecting to notice a huge change in his appearance, but he looked the same. If I hadn't be told about his addiction, I probably would have never known. His eyes still had that charmer sparkle, and he was still the big, curly-haired giant I had known since high school.

He opened the passenger door and said, "What's up Casper?" Referring to my pigmentation.

He jumped into my truck and we went through the drive-thru of

Whataburger. We pulled over on the side of the road and ate on the hood of my truck like we used to when we were in high school.

When we were done, I wasn't exactly sure how I was going to get him back to Abilene, so I just started driving in that direction, hoping he wouldn't notice we were leaving town right away. It took me a couple of minutes to decide what to tell him.

Eventually, I said, "Matt... I'm not taking you back home man."

He looked over at me in disbelief, "What? What do you mean?"

"I'm sorry. I know about your addiction and it has to stop. I'm bringing you back to Abilene with me."

"What?" He positioned his body to get a better look at me, probably trying to figure out if I was being serious.

"Yeah man, I'm not taking you back home. You're not going back," I replied sternly.

At the time there wasn't Uber or Lyft, and Matt didn't have the money to take a taxi even if he wanted to, so he was stuck with me. I guess he could have walked, but that was unlikely since we'd be a four-hour drive away. After a couple of minutes of silence, he agreed to come with me. Matt knew he had a problem, and I was glad he was willing to accept my help.

"Before we leave though, let's go out one last time," he said. He must have seen the unimpressed look on my face because he quickly followed up with, "Just so I can see everyone, one last time. I promise I'll go back with you to Abilene."

I stayed quiet, trying to process his request.

"Come on Roy. You can't just drive me to another city without saying goodbye to my friends. You know I have other friends, right? Just let me say goodbye to them and I promise I'll go with you."

I should have said no, but I didn't.

I replied, "Alright, fine. We'll go out."

I took the first exit and headed back towards downtown. He didn't even have to call his friends, the chances of them being at the bar were likely. As we pulled up, I told him we'd only stay for a little bit and then we were going to leave. Despite not wanting to go out, I had a great time catching up with some of our mutual friends. Everything seemed to be going smoothly until I looked over and saw Matt with George, who I figured was his coke dealer due to his reputation in the local area. They were standing in the corner talking. I quickly walked up to them, barely hearing what they were saying, when Matt turned to me and said, "I'll be right back."

I raised my eyebrows, dropped my head, and shook it ever so slightly then fixed my eyes on Matt's.

"I don't know man, I think you should stay here. It's not a goo—"

"Damn! I said I'll be right back, Roy!" he said as he walked out of the bar, leaving me standing alone.

As I walked back to my stool I thought, *I knew I shouldn't have brought him here. How could you be so stupid, Roy?*

I sat back down on the stools and continued talking to one of our mutual friends, Javier. We got caught up in conversation and before I knew it, 30 minutes had passed. I scanned the bar and still no sign of Matt. *Where the hell was he?*

"Excuse me really quick, I think Matt's outside. I'm gonna go check on him, we're supposed to be leaving here soon," I said to Javier as I got up from the stool.

I walked through the front doors and was confronted with a slew of flashing red and blue lights from across the street. About eight cop cars were surrounding an all-white vehicle.

I began scanning the crowd that had formed, looking for Matt. Still, no sign of him. I hoped he didn't leave with George, I should have never brought him here. Just then, there was a break in the crowd and still on the ground against the all-white vehicle was Matt. I moved forward to take a closer look. He was in handcuffs! I thought, *Oh $%&#! That must be George's car!*

Unsure of what I should do, I got into my car and parked it in a spot where I could watch what was happening. I pulled out my flip phone and called my sister Tammy.

"Tammy, Tammy can you hear me?" I said frantically.

I must have startled her because I could tell in her voice she had just woken up. "Roy, what's wrong? Is everything okay?" She asked.

"Matt and I came out, and I'm not sure what happened, but he's sitting on the ground handcuffed outside, surrounded by the cops."

"Wait, what? Where are you?"

"We're downtown, we came out and Matt left with his dealer. Now he's surrounded by cops, I can see him sitting on the ground in handcuffs. I dunno what to do!"

"LEAVE. You need to leave Roy before they think you're a part of it. He made his choice! Leave."

"But what about Matt? I don't want to be a bad friend."

"You can't help him now. You need to leave before you get in trouble too! If you try to help him and the cops think you're a part of whatever's going on, it's over for you. You have to go, it's not you being a bad friend Roy. You can't help others if they aren't willing to help themselves. Leave!" Tammy demanded.

Still feeling guilty, I started driving away from the scene. I was so close to helping Matt, and now it was all down the drain. I felt dumb and guilty for letting him convince me to go out "one last time." Five minutes into my drive, my phone started ringing. I glanced at the screen, and to my surprise, it was Matt calling! I quickly answered.

"Oh my god, oh my god, come pick me up. Come pick me up!" he said in a panic.

"Where are you? Are you still across the street from the bar?"

"Yes! Hurry hurry! Oh my god I can't believe they let me go. I'm outside waiting. Hurry! I can't believe they let me go!"

I turned the car around at once and headed back to the scene. Sure enough, I saw Matt walking down the street, away from the bar. I pulled up next to him, and he jumped in.

I didn't even give him time to shut the door before asking, "What the hell happened, Matt?"

"Roy, I swear to you I didn't even get a chance to do anything. I had just got into the car with George. We were only going to do a couple bumps, but when he lifted up the baggy and flicked it; the cops rushed us. We didn't even know he was being watched. I swear! But when they rushed us, I had a baggie in my hand. I couldn't let them catch me with it, so I swallowed it," he spoke fast, still shaken up from what had happened.

"You what?" I asked, sounding like an upset parent.

"I swallowed it. I didn't know what else to do!"

"Matt, what the hell? Are you stupid? If that baggie opens up, you're screwed! Oh my gosh. I need to take you to the hospital or something."

"Are you crazy Roy?! You can't take me to the damn hospital!"

I didn't know what to do. I decided to call our mutual friend, Nano Montelongo, who was an emergency room nurse in Los Angeles. I was surprised he even picked up.

"Hey Nano, sorry it's late, but I have a very important question. A medical question."

"It's okay Roy, I'm just at home watching some movies. What's going on? Is everything okay?"

I took a deep breath. "Well, one of my friends swallowed a small baggie of cocaine," I said, trying to hide Matt's identity. "I'm just concerned about what might happen if the bag were to open up inside him."

"Is it Matt?" Nano asked.

I hesitated for a second, looked over at Matt, then said, "Yeah, it is."

"How often he does he use?"

I turned to Matt and asked, "How often do you use?"

He stayed quiet.

"How often do you use?!" I repeated myself, raising my voice.

"Every day."

My friend was in bigger trouble than I had thought.

"He said every day, Nano."

"Oh. Well, he'll be fine. Just keep an eye on him."

"Okay, he'll be fine? I don't have to take him to the hospital?"

"If he's using every day, like with any drug, the first time you use it, it tears you up. Your body builds a tolerance. You need more to get the same effect. If he's using every day, he will be fine."

"Thanks man, thanks for your help. Sorry again for calling so late," I said, feeling embarrassed.

"Anytime. Be careful out there, Roy."

"Thanks," I replied as I hung up the phone.

I changed direction away from the hospital, and continued the drive straight to Abilene, without saying a word.

I hid Matt in my dorm room, which was against school policy. For at least two weeks, we were sneaking him in and out. After just a couple of days, I could tell he was having withdrawals. He hated being there. Without a car or money, there was nothing for him to do but sit around all day in my room. As tension grew between us, and he grew antsier, I worried that he might actually do something to get caught on purpose. Once again, I called my older sister Tammy for advice.

"Roy, I know he's one of your best friends, and we all love him like a brother, but you can't have him there with you. It's too much of a risk, especially after all the work you've put in to get into college. Could you imagine if you got caught? What if they kicked you out of school?"

"Yeah... trust me, I've thought about that already. I just don't want to take him back home, and then he ends up in the same situation or worse," I sighed.

"Look, why don't you send him to me? I'll watch over him. I've known him long enough and I rather he stays here with me than you risk everything."

"Uh, are you sure Tammy? I mean he's not your responsibility..."

"Well he's not yours either, Roy. Just fly him out here to Vegas and I'll let him stay with me," she proposed.

"Alright," I replied. "Deal."

After we got off the phone, I booked Matt's flight for the following week. When the day finally came, I drove him to the airport and wished him good luck.

He lived with my sister for 8 months, rent-free. Tammy had her daughter give up her bedroom, so Matt would have his own personal space to help him withdraw from his cocaine habit. Even after, when Matt still wasn't financially stable, he moved in with Mrs. K for another 8 months, rent-free. She eventually offered him a job and helped him get his first apartment.

I helped Matt because I loved him like a brother. He didn't owe me anything, but I was still shocked that he wasn't willing to help me when I needed it. I was back at Nick's house, packing up the last of my belongings when I started to realize that maybe our friendship had been more one-sided than I thought.

The next morning, I went back to the Kickbusch house and Mrs. K told me that she had a meeting with her husband and Matt the night before. They decided to terminate his position but gave him a five-month notice as a way to help him out. A part of me felt responsible for his termination, but she reassured me that he had it coming as his recent work ethic was declining.

We briefly talked at the kitchen table before she suggested we take a drive. We got in the car and she insisted on driving. To my surprise, she took me to an extended stay hotel.

She said, "Mijo, I have a solution to your housing problem. Don't worry, you're not going to be homeless. Well, not until the tour starts up again."

We walked into the hotel, and Mrs. K said to the receptionist, "I need to book a room for two weeks."

The receptionist replied, "Not a problem. Let me see what we have."

After typing into her computer, she continued, "Okay ma'am, I have you down for one room for two weeks. Your total comes out to $2,127, including tax."

I felt like such a burden! Of course, this gesture alone wasn't satisfying enough for my mentor. When we got back into her car, she drove me to Target.

"We need to buy you everything you need. These extended stays don't have the necessities. We need to buy pots, pans, bed sheets, dish soap…"

The more she listed, the worse I felt. We spent about an hour at Target before we had everything I "needed." As we headed back to the extended stay, she answered a phone call and immediately started freaking out.

"Ay Dios Mio, is he okay? Are you sure? Oh my goodness," she looked over at me with a worried expression.

"What's wrong? Is everything okay?"

She pulled the phone away from her face, "It's Matt's roommate, Desiree. She said he tried committing suicide this morning!"

I rolled my eyes, "Ma'am, no he didn't. Give me the phone."

Mrs. K handed me the phone, and with anger in my voice, I said, "Desiree, this is Roy. I have two questions for you. How drunk was he? And how sharp was the knife?"

"Well, he was really drunk. He drank an entire bottle of Vodka last night, and he probably wasn't going to make it to work… Thankfully, the knife was only a butter knife…" his roommate replied.

I didn't bother listening to anything else she had to say. I pulled the phone away from my ear and handed it back to Mrs. K. I knew Matt wasn't going to hurt himself. I've known him for years and this was just another one of his manipulative moves. I was so pissed off at him and had no clue what the hell his problem was! It wasn't even a cry for help, he was still drunk from partying the night before. Since he was already in trouble at work, he needed a good enough reason why he couldn't come in. In a drunken stupor, he figured an "attempted suicide with a butter knife" would suffice.

Even though I was furious and didn't want to see him, I knew my mentor wanted to check up on him, so we drove straight to his apartment. When we arrived, there were two cop cars parked outside. I made my way towards his front door while Mrs. K stayed outside to call her husband and update him on the situation.

As I approached his apartment, the front door was already opened. I walked right in and down the hall into the living room to see Matt sitting on the edge of his couch, hunched over, talking to one of the cops.

The cop noticed me walk in and asked, "Are you a friend or family?"

"I'm a friend, sir."

"What's your name?"

"My name is Roy, sir," I answered.

The cop turned towards Matt, "Is this the Roy guy you don't want in your apartment?"

He looked up from the edge of the couch, his eyes bloodshot, and his face drenched in sweat. "Yeah, that's him," he replied, looking me dead in the eye.

I broke our eye contact, thought to myself, *this is so stupid,* turned back towards the cop, and threw my hands up slightly, "Not a problem, I'll leave sir. Thank you."

As I walked back out the front door, my mentor was about to step in. Surprised to see me walking out she asked, "What's wrong, is he okay?"

"Yeah, he's in there, he doesn't want me in his apartment."

"What?" She asked in confusion as she quickly walked past me to make her way inside.

I waited outside not knowing what the hell was going on with my "best friend." After about ten minutes of sitting on the curb, an ambulance pulled up and made their way into the apartment. Moments later, they brought Matt out on a stretcher. Everyone slowly followed behind him.

Once the last of the cops left, I went inside. Even though Matt was a jerk with me, I still loved him like a brother. I grabbed his phone and the keys to lock up. I knew something wasn't right with him and wanted desperately to find out what it was. So, I decided to go through his phone to gain insight, hoping to find an answer.

Everything in Matt's phone appeared to be normal, there was nothing out of the ordinary... Until I came across one of his text messages with a mutual friend of ours. As I was scrolling through the conversation, I couldn't believe what I was reading. Messages from Matt read, "I &@%#ing hate Roy!" "He needs to get out of Vegas already." "He's such a %@#$!" "Why is he even here?" My mouth dropped, and I got a horrible feeling in the pit of my stomach. *What did I ever do to him?* I was so angry, and I needed to vent to someone, so I called my sister Tammy to tell her what happened.

I couldn't bear to see Matt after what I had read, so instead, I gave my mentor his phone before we parted ways for the day. I headed back to Nick's house to keep packing up my things. I wanted to make sure everything ready to be moved into my mentor's garage before I went to the extended stay.

The next day, while I was looking through my boxes, I heard a buzzing noise a couple of feet away. I looked over at my phone, the caller ID read "Matt." As much as I didn't want to answer, I picked up the phone anyway. I stayed quiet until he finally said something.

"Hey Roy," he said. I could hear the uncertainty in his voice.

"Hey Matt," I mirrored his greeting.

"How are you?" he asked.

"I think the real question is, how are *you?*"

"I'm still in the hospital, but I wanted to call to see if you could pick me up."

"Naw man, I can't. Sorry," I replied, annoyed that he would even ask.

"It's cool. Well, I also wanted to apologize."

"For what?"

"My roommate told me how rude I was to you when I was drunk. I figured it was true because Tammy also sent me a hateful message on Facebook."

"Matt, Tammy wasn't mad at you for what you said to me when you were drunk. She was mad at you for what you said about me when you were sober."

"When I was sober?" He asked confused.

"Yeah man. I went through your phone to try and figure out what the hell's going on with you, and I saw your text messages. What you wrote about me. How you said you hated me and that I was a %#&@."

There was an awkward silence.

"Well, I'm not going to apologize because I said it," he said carelessly.

"That's fine. I'm not asking you to apologize to me. I hope you have a great life." I hung up the phone.

I'm not sure if he had anything else he wanted to say, but I didn't want to hear it. This situation was now the least of my worries. I still had my new traveling assistant coming into town, and the tour would be starting in two weeks.

# CHAPTER ELEVEN

## Are You Kidding Me?

THE DAY FINALLY came when Kenny flew into town. I could see him walking out of the airport area and into the baggage claim where I was waiting for him. He was a pretty big guy. He was broad and looked intimidating. I thought, *People are going to think I hired a bodyguard for the tour.* I chuckled to myself as I walked up to him.

From the airport, we drove straight to Phoenix, Arizona for my event, where I would be speaking at the Aguila Youth Symposium. Kenny's responsibilities were the same as any of my other traveling assistants; he'd drive the car, take pictures at the event, identify key individuals, and if we were given the opportunity, sell wristbands.

During the event, Kenny did a great job of working and staying on task. Everything ran smoothly, and he interacted well with the clients, but for some reason, I didn't have a connection with him. See, the biggest thing I was looking for was compatibility. All of the other things it took to be my assistant could be learned, but not a connection. While on tour I didn't want, nor did I have the time, to build a friendship. I needed something that clicked instantly.

It wasn't until our drive back to Vegas that I realized things really weren't going to work out with Kenny joining me on tour. The car ride was awkward, and I knew after being with him for the last several hours, I wouldn't enjoy his company for months at a time. As we drove closer to the city, I tried to figure out a way to tell Kenny it wasn't going to work out. Although I knew our personalities weren't compatible, I felt horrible breaking the news to him within 24 hours of our meeting, so I decided to wait till the next morning to say anything.

Early in the morning, I took Kenny to a Starbucks close by our extended stay.

"Kenny, I'm gonna be honest with you, I don't think this is going to work out. There's nothing you did wrong, it just isn't going to work. I feel like we aren't compatible and that's a big factor I was looking for," I sounded as though I was breaking up with him. "You can spend the rest of the week here with me if you want. You don't have to do anything, and I'll still pay you for the week since you took the time to come. You can consider this as a vacation," I said, hoping I at least came across as nice as possible. Surprisingly, he didn't have an adverse reaction and agreed to hang out in Vegas while I prepared for the second phase of the tour.

After a couple of days of working in the hotel, I decided to change up the scenery and work at my mentor's house to have some privacy while also giving Kenny his space. I was there for most of the day but I didn't want to impose on her kindness by asking to stay the night as well, so I went back to the hotel. When I got to the room, the dirty pile of clothes I had thrown on the bed that morning was still waiting for me. I grabbed the coin-filled sock that was in my dresser drawer to get some quarters for the hotel washer and dryer. As soon as I lifted it up from my bag, I noticed it was much lighter.

*That's weird*, I thought.

My hand dug into the sock, but I couldn't feel any quarters. I peeked inside, still nothing. I emptied the coins out on to the bed, and all the silver coins were gone. *Was this kid really stealing from me?*

I walked into the living room and asked, "Hey Kenny, did you use some of my coins for laundry?"

"No. Why, is something wrong?" he replied.

"Well, I've been saving my coins for toll roads on tour, but all my silver is missing." I tried to play it off by saying, "Oh well, I must have put it somewhere else," as I walked back into the bedroom.

But I knew my coins were in my sock, which meant Kenny was most likely stealing from me. I had a plan to find out. I put my empty sock back into my drawer and walked into the living room to watch T.V., pretending nothing was wrong. As I sat across the room from him, it was killing me inside because I knew what he had done. I just needed proof.

About 30 minutes later, I looked over at Kenny and asked, "Kenny, you hungry?"

"Uh, yeah, a little bit."

"I saw a pizza place on the way back here. If I buy, you fly? I'm only asking cause I'm tired," I hoped he would take the bait.

He got up from the couch, "Yeah, for sure, that's fine. Just get me the address, and I'll go. Thanks for paying."

I gave Kenny the address and waited a couple of minutes for him to get in the car. I watched through the window and made sure he left before I sprang into action. I grabbed his suitcase and placed it on the edge of the bed. I felt crazy for going through his belongings, but I needed to be sure he wasn't stealing from me. Slowly, I unpacked his stuff, making sure not to unfold his clothes, just in case he was innocent. After moving a few things, I didn't see my coins, but I saw my camera and pocket knife! I was pissed. I knew something was up. I went through his bag looking for my coins but how could I care about a few bucks when he had my camera?! Now, I didn't care about moving his crap around. I finally found my coins in a unique handmade bag my friend from Russia had given me.

I. Was. Furious.

How could this guy steal from me after I offered him a paid week in Vegas where he had ZERO work to do? I was disappointed, but not surprised. I was literally just screwed over by my best friend days before! This had to be one of my worst weeks since the tour had started.

Halfway through planning how I would approach him when he got back to the hotel, my phone started to ring.

I answered, "Hey Kenny, everything alright?"

"Not really. I can't find the pizza place, I think my GPS isn't working or something. Do you want me to just pick up something else?" he asked.

"Just come back to the hotel, and I'll go with you to the place. I remember where it's at. Let me know when you're outside," I told him as we hung up. Now I had to rethink my plan. How would I bring it up?

Kenny finally made it back to the hotel to pick me up.

When I walked outside, I said, "Hey, let me drive."

"I don't mind driving," he replied.

"Naw, I wanna drive."

He got out of the driver seat, and I took over. We drove straight to the pizza place. Once we picked up the pizza, I had him hold it in his lap as we made our way back to the hotel. We were just blocks away when I noticed the car was low on gas. I pulled into the closest gas station, realizing this was the perfect opportunity to confront Kenny. He was much bigger than I was, but at least now he was sitting down in the car, with his seatbelt on, and holding the pizza box in his hands. If by any chance he wanted to get physical, he wouldn't be as quick with all the barriers between us.

As the gas was pumping, I walked over to the passenger side of the car and leaned into the window.

"So… why'd you take my change?" I said without hesitation.

The look on his face when I asked gave him away.

"What? I didn't, I didn't take your stuff. I didn't take your change," he stuttered.

From my pocket, I pulled out one of the belongings I found in his suitcase, the handmade bag I was gifted. "Oh really? Then what's this?" I asked, holding it up in his face.

"WHAT! You went through my bag? How coul—"

"No! You need to stop right there!" I pointed in his face, "You need to find somewhere else to stay because you're NOT staying with me. If you find somewhere to stay, I won't cancel your flight back home, BUT, if you don't find somewhere to stay tonight, I'm gonna cancel your flight, and you can find your own way back home."

We drove back to the hotel in silence, and I waited the rest of the night for him to tell me where he was going to stay. After several hours, he stood in the doorway of the hotel bedroom and confessed he couldn't find anywhere.

I had already figured he wouldn't be able to, considering we were in a city where he didn't know anyone.

"Okay. I'll get you a hotel, but don't think you're getting rewarded or anything like that, because I'm doing this for me. I don't want you around me, and I definitely don't want you in the same hotel," I paused for a moment. "Also, your card will be put down for incidentals so if you mess up the room, it's on you. Go get your stuff and let's go."

I drove to a hotel close to the airport, checked him in, thanked the lady at the front desk and walked out. I didn't tell him goodbye or even look at him as I left. Kenny only lasted four days, and that was the last time I'd have someone on tour with me who I didn't know personally. After I made it back to the hotel, a traveling assistant was the furthest thing from my mind. I was over it, and ready to start phase two of the tour by myself.

## James Joins the Tour

I called my best friend, James Alvarez, to vent about what happened with Matt and Kenny. I always kept him updated on things that were going on with the tour. I'm sure he felt sorry for me because he offered to be my next traveling assistant if I needed one. Although I was tired of losing people, he was one of my best friends, so I kept him in mind.

A couple of days passed when he texted me asking, "Do you need my help or not?"

I reviewed the tour route and knew I needed his help. If he came with me, that meant he would have to quit his job and move out of his girlfriend's house. Part of me didn't want to put him in that position, but I replied honestly.

"Bro, I really do need you."

We decided he'd meet me in Vegas the following week.

Within a few days, we came up with a bulletproof plan. I would sell my car, use that money for the tour, and we'd drive his car instead. James had already quit his job working as a Prevention Specialist, so I knew he wouldn't back out. I continued to prepare him via phone calls on what the tour would be like, and what he'd need to do. Finally, the day came where he pulled into the driveway of my mentor's house in Vegas.

Once he parked and got out of his car I asked, "What happened to your hair?"

He laughed, "I got tired of it! Plus, I save a lot of money with it like this."

"You look like Mr. Clean," I said as I rubbed his bald head.

"You look like the Pillsbury Doughboy," he said as he poked my stomach.

"This is how you're going to look once the tour is over. I'm telling you, it's hard to eat healthy on the road."

"Sheeeeze, my body will look even better."

We both laughed.

"So, where's my first paycheck?"

"You're fired, jerk."

He laughed, "Mijo, don't be so mean! Naw, I'm glad I could make it out here with you."

I gave him a hug, showed him inside, and we caught up the entire evening since it would be our only free night for a while. We had planned to be on the road by 4:30 am the next morning to start our trip to Anaheim, California for my first presentation. I was scheduled to speak at Sunkist Community Church and didn't want to run late.

During the drive to the event, I realized how thankful I was for my best friend. If it weren't for him, I wouldn't have gotten an extra five hours of sleep while he drove. When we arrived at Sunkist Community Church, we were greeted by Pastor Jorge Herrera, a slender man with thinning brownish-grey hair, who had previously heard me speak.

"Roy, it's great to see you again. I'm glad you could make it..." Pastor Herrera said with a tone of excitement. "Here's how the morning will go; I'll do the praise and worship, some announcements, you'll speak, and then I'll close with a recap on the message," he spoke with authority.

"Sounds great, Pastor Jorge. Where would you like us to sit during the praise and worship?" I asked.

"The both of you can sit right in the first pew," he said as we walked into the sanctuary.

As Pastor Jorge spoke, I felt glad to be sitting through a church service. On tour, unless I was scheduled to speak at a church, I didn't really have time to go and enjoy it. From the corner of my eye, I could see James fighting to stay awake. He was exhausted from his first drive on tour. I nudged him as I got up to speak.

Once I finished sharing my message, Pastor Jorge went up to summarize it. I was touched by what he said before he closed the service.

"…Now, we're going to pick up a love offering. We only have one bag being passed around, so please be patient. As you decide to donate, I want you to think about what Roy has said and what it means for you personally. He's out here doing a great thing that I think we can all stand behind," he looked at me and smiled. "As the love offering is being picked up, I'd like for you, Mr. Juarez and James, to come up here so we can pray a special blessing upon you for your journey."

The congregation members all stood up, extended their hands and prayed over us. I thanked everyone one last time, and the service came to an end. I stayed in the front, watching the members make their way out of the sanctuary. As I waved everyone out, a young couple approached me. They both personally thanked me for speaking at the service, but then the young woman stepped out of the aisle and moved closer to me.

"We aren't huge fans of coming to church," she said, pointing to her boyfriend. "This morning when my mom called me to make sure I was coming, I honestly just wanted to tell her I wasn't feeling well to get out of meeting her here. Church isn't my thing, but the story you told us today really touched me. So, thank you. Thank you for coming today because you made me glad that I came after all," she smiled.

I stood there in awe. "Well, thank you," I replied. "What you said makes me feel like I'm doing something right."

While the young couple said their goodbyes, I noticed a woman lingering behind them. As they walked away, she approached me.

"Hi, my name's Rachel. I was wondering if you could do me a huge favor," she said softly.

Nervous of what she might ask of me, I replied with caution, "Well ma'am, I can certainly try. What can I help you with?"

"My son is in prison, and it would mean a lot to me if you could write to him, maybe tell him your story," she replied.

"I'd be happy to ma'am. I'll give you my information, so you can give it to your son. Tell him as soon as I receive his letter, I'll take the time to reply."

She thanked me, took down my information and walked away. Behind her, there was a line of congregation members ready to tell me their story and thank me for sharing mine. By the time I conversed with all of them, 30 minutes had passed. I looked over and saw Pastor Jorge and James wrapping up their conversation and walking towards me from the altar.

"You did great today Roy, I could tell you touched many people with your message," said Pastor Jorge.

"Thank you sir, I wouldn't have been able to do it without you allowing me here," I smiled. Just as I was about to say goodbye, he turned around and walked back to the altar.

"You don't wanna forget this," he said holding up the love offering, still inside the bag. "We don't wanna know how much money we collected for your tour, so just take it all."

He placed the bag in my hand and leaned in for a hug.

I embraced him back while saying, "Thank you so much for everything, Pastor Jorge. I truly feel blessed today."

We both said one last goodbye and headed back to the car. I could tell James was still tired, so I suggested he take a quick nap while I drove. That evening we didn't have a place to stay. I suggested we sleep in the car, but James said, "I'll be your host family. I just received my last paycheck from my other job. I'll get us a hotel." I wasn't going to say no to my best friend if he was trying to bless me. That would be rude!

With nothing to do that evening, we decided to visit some friends I had met during the first phase of the tour. We drove to the World Impact youth group meeting in South Central, Los Angeles. The kids were surprised to see me since I showed up unannounced. I was giving them hugs when they insisted I needed to meet the speaker for the evening.

A young lady with a familiar face approached me and said, "Hi, I'm April. Nice to meet you."

I recognized her, but I wasn't sure where from. Her naturally curly hair and well-manicured eyebrows complimented her rosy cheeks and velvet black eyes. In the end, it didn't matter, we hit it off and start talking about life. We talked until it was time for her to address the youth group. In her presentation, she shared her experiences as an activist and actress.

*Actress?* I thought. Where do I know her from? Then it clicked! I know who she is… she played "Eva" in one of my favorite movies, Freedom Writers, produced by Danny DeVito, Michael Shamberg and Stacey Sher in 2007. I was ecstatic to meet her.

The evening ended on a high note. After we left World Impact, James and I went back to the hotel, to rest and prepare for the presentations that week. L.A. flew by, and before we knew it, it was time to head North.

As we were driving to San Francisco, California, we received a call.

"Good afternoon Mr. Juarez, we heard you were in the area, and we would really like you to speak to our students."

"Thank you, are you in Los Angeles or the Bay Area?"

"We are located in Los Angeles."

"Thank you so much for reaching out to me, but my tour already left the L.A. area. I'm currently heading up to San Francisco," I replied.

The lady on the other end of the phone insisted I return, "Please sir? Our students really need to hear your message. Also, the school is willing to offer a donation to your tour as well."

"One-second ma'am," I muted the phone and looked over at James who was driving, "You aren't going to like me right now."

"I never did," he said jokingly.

I took the phone off mute, "Ma'am, I'm only available tomorrow morning. If that works for you, I'm willing to make my way back to L.A."

"Oh, thank you sir. We will make it work! I'll send you an email later today with all the information you'll need to get to our campus," she said.

We exchanged our goodbyes and hung up.

James looked over at me rolling his eyes, "Let me guess. We're driving back to L.A.?"

"Yup! But before you say anything else, the school is willing to give a donation to help the tour. Right now, you know we could really use it." I hoped this was enough to convince him as to why we needed to turn back around. He grabbed the GPS and typed in Los Angeles, California.

"Well, we need to fill up," he said and pulled in to the closest gas station. We filled up the tank, which wasn't cheap, and began our drive south. Halfway to L.A., I reached out to my friend Jason Carrier to ask if we could stay with him again. Thankfully, he said yes.

The day of the event was exciting. My new friends Jason Carrier, April Lee Hernandez and her husband, Jose Castillo, had agreed to join us.

We all arrived at the school, and the secretary led me to a large classroom setting. There weren't any desks or chairs in the room, so all the students were sitting close together on the floor. I guess this was a good thing because the number of students who were there wouldn't have fit otherwise. The presentation ended up going extremely well, the students were receptive to my message. Staying true to their word, before we left the campus, the school handed James an envelope with our donation. As we all started walking to our car, James burst out laughing.

"What's so funny man?" I asked.

Still laughing he replied, "I'll tell you when we get in the car."

As soon as we got in the car, he handed me the envelope.

"Okay? But what's so funny?" I asked again as I started to open it.

"We spent more on gas than they gave us in the donation," James said.

I looked in the envelope and stared at the $50 check the school had donated. I took a deep breath and thought about our situation; the tour was already short on funds. James and I spent more money driving back to L.A. than we made.

James interrupted my thoughts by asking, "Well, now that we have all this money, where are we headed?"

"Since we're rich, we're going to eat with the $50 the school just donated!" I said sarcastically. "No but seriously, I already told Jason, April, and Jose that we'd meet them at Mel's Diner in Hollywood. Here's the address," I said as I handed James my cell phone. He started the GPS, and we were off.

During our lunch, Jason offered his couch to us for another night so we could rest before leaving town.

"Well, I don't know Jason… If we leave in the morning we would have to be on the road by 3:00 am to get to our next event on time. We're headed out to Eugene, Oregon remember?" I knew I needed to rest, but staying the night meant running the risk we wouldn't make it to our next event. I looked over at James, I could tell from the bags under his eyes that he was just as exhausted as I was. Before Jason could respond, I said, "But you know what? You're right, we do need to rest before we get on the road again. We'll stay another night." I was able to read James' face correctly because as soon as I said we'd stay, I saw him look relieved.

We finished our lunch, said our goodbyes to April and Jose, then followed Jason back to his apartment.

During the car ride, James started a conversation in a serious tone, saying, "Hey Roy, I don't know how to say this… but, I can't do this anymore man."

I quickly turned my body to face him and asked, "What are you talking about?"

He replied slowly, "This. I can't live like… this. I don't want to live like this. I miss my life, my girlfriend, consistency. I wanna to go home."

"Are you serious right now? James, I JUST sold my car because you told me we could use yours when you came on tour with me!"

My voice was rising with every word I said, but I made a conscious effort to at least control it a bit. I took a deep breath before I continued, "Look, if you leave, I won't have a car, which means, I won't have a tour. Can you please just wait until I get another car?"

"Roy, I didn't say I was leaving right now. I can do this for another couple of weeks…" he said.

We sat in silence for the rest of the ride, but my mind was racing to find a solution. *What was I going to do? How would I make it work?* Silently, I prayed for help. As always, God was right on time.

I received a text message from my sister Tammy that read, "Roy, I forgot to tell you. I checked the P.O. Box and you received a $5,000 check, I deposited it this morning."

"Seriously?!? From who?" I replied.

My sister informed me it was from a well-known soda company. Once I heard the name, I knew exactly who had sent me the check. I called my friend, Frank, and thanked him.

He responded, "Roy, we don't usually give money to individuals, but we believe in what you're doing. We don't want any recognition, don't put it on social media, just take the money and keep making a difference."

A huge burden lifted off me. Now, I needed to find a car. And quick.

The next morning, James and I were on the road by 3:00 am and I still hadn't told him about the check. We headed North to Eugene, Oregon and were determined to get as close as possible before we stopped driving. I kept checking my account to see if the funds were available. Halfway to the Bay Area, I checked again, and sitting in my account was the $5,000. Quickly, I called my friend in San Francisco and asked if she knew of anyone selling a car.

"Hmmm… I think my brother Ed is, but he lives up in Petaluma. Let me give you his number, and I'll let him know you're gonna reach out to him."

Sure enough, when I contacted Ed, he confirmed he was selling a Nissan Altima and was willing to let me stop by to test drive it. I grabbed the GPS and punched in our new destination.

James asked, "Man, why are we gonna look at a car? We don't have any money. I told you I don't have to leave now, I can stay a little longer."

With a huge smile, I said, "We got a check for $5,000 yesterday and Tammy deposited it. The funds hit our account about twenty minutes ago."

"Dude that's awesome! Man, God always has your back, it's insane."

When we arrived and got out of the car, a man walked out of the garage, and asked, "Are you Roy?" We walked over to introduce ourselves, and as Ed wiped his hands with an old rag, he said, "I was waiting for you guys, nice to meet you." I shook his hand and followed him to the car. "This is the only one I have at the moment," he said pointing to a silver Nissan Altima.

"It looks good, how much are you asking for it?" I asked.

"Right now, it's sitting at $5,500, and I don't think I'll go any lower than that Roy," Ed replied.

I tried to hide the fact that it was a bit out of my price range, "Okay great, that's perfect. Do you think I can test drive it really quick before I make my decision?"

He reached into his pocket, "I knew you'd ask. Here are the keys, you can take it around the block for a bit and let me know what you think."

"Do you need to hold on to my ID or something?" I asked.

"Naw, you're good. My sister told me about your tour and why you need the car. I trust you," Ed replied. "Now go take it for a spin!"

"Thank you sir, but I have one more question. Would it be possible to pay you $2,500 now and the rest in payments?" I reluctantly asked. I hoped this wouldn't change whether or not he'd sell me the car.

He stood there quietly, processing the favor I had asked. Finally, he answered, "Yeah, I guess that's fine, but just know I don't usually do it that way."

"You're awesome Ed! I really appreciate it," I thanked him and turned to James, "Come on James, let's test drive it."

We got in the car, and before I had a chance to start it, I could sense something was wrong with James when he said, "Man! I feel bad! I feel bad for leaving you like this. I feel like a quitter," he said.

I looked at James with a straight face. "You're not a quitter... You're just weak!" He looked over at me with wide eyes, and I couldn't help but bust out laughing.

"You're a jerk, Roy!" he said and started laughing with me. To this day, I still joke with him; you're not a quitter, you're just weak.

Finally, I started the car and instructed James to double check all of the buttons and make sure they worked. I drove around the block a couple of times then went straight to Wells Fargo and withdrew $3,000. I planned to give $2,500 as the down payment for the car, and $500 to get James back to Dallas, Texas.

When we arrived back at Ed's place, I exchanged the money I withdrew for the paperwork in his hands and an extra set of car keys. It was now about noon, and I wanted to have one last lunch with James before we went our separate ways. He followed me around downtown Petaluma until I found a pizza place I knew we'd both enjoy. We sat in the restaurant for a couple of hours, laughing about the moments we had lived through in college. Neither of us wanted to stop reminiscing, but it was getting late, and I needed to get back on the road.

We walked out to our cars and James apologized one last time before we hugged and said our goodbyes. Just as he was getting into his car, I heard him call out, "Hey Roy, I hope I can join you again on your tour sometime. Maybe next time I won't be so weak." We both laughed and got into our cars. He headed back to Dallas, and I continued my drive North for Eugene, Oregon.

# CHAPTER TWELVE

## I Don't Blame You

### Eugene, Oregon - 8 Months into the Tour

I WOKE UP in a panic. *Had I slept through my alarm?* The drive north, up Route 1 took me longer than expected due to the dense fog, so I decided to pull over in Florence, Oregon for a two-hour nap before continuing my trip. I reached over to the passenger seat, scrambling for my phone. The time read 6:07 am, pretty much right on schedule. I threw some water from my bottle into my hands and splashed my face. Only an hour and a half left until I would reach my destination.

When I finally made it to town, the first people I met with were John Crowder and Ken Harvey. John was an older man, several inches taller than I was, with short ivory hair and wire-framed glasses. Ken, also an older gentleman, was broad, with light brown hair, and an impressive mustache that reminded me of Mario from Nintendo®. These men had helped organize my stay in Eugene and also oversaw the Hosea Homeless Drop-In Center, one of the places I would be speaking. We first met for breakfast to become acquainted and review the presentations I had lined up during my stay.

"Okay Roy, the first stop we have is New Hope Christian College. You'll be speaking there in a couple of hours and then right after we're heading over to Cascade Middle School for another presentation," John explained.

We finished up breakfast and headed over to the college. Around 100 people showed up, and the presentation went fantastically. The high energy of the audience stayed with me, and I was excited to speak at the middle school next. On the drive over, John and Ken warned me that the school was hesitant to let me speak, but it wasn't the first time I had heard that, so I kept my positive energy. They dropped me off and reminded me that John's son would be waiting for me afterward.

As I walked into the front office of Cascade, the secretary stood up from behind her desk and walked over to greet me. "Hi welcome in, how can I help you?" she asked.

I stepped up to the front desk to introduce myself. "Hello there, I'm Roy Juarez Jr., I'm here for a presentation."

"Oh, yes! Mr. Juarez, I'm so glad you're here," she said with a smile.

"Of course ma'am," I replied. "Also, I just wanted to say thank you so much for giving me the opportunity to speak."

"Aren't we lucky? Well, let me go ahead and show you where the cafeteria is, that's where you'll give your presentation," she said as we walked out of the front office. "Also, I was told I needed to talk to you about something having to do with your story… but first, let's get you settled in. This way."

I was confused by her comment, *What did she need to speak with me about?* We headed over to the cafeteria and just before we got to the stage she stopped and turned towards me. "Mr. Juarez, we are pleased to have you here to speak to our students. We absolutely love what you're doing… but the administration would prefer if you didn't talk about homelessness, at all."

My jaw almost hit the floor. *How was I supposed to tell my story while leaving out the part where I became homeless?* "Um, ma'am, that's a big part of my message. I'm not sure if the students will get the same outcome without me mentioning it." I hoped she would see my side of things without me having to be too pushy.

"Well, I'm sure you can find a way to tell your story without mentioning it. We just don't want the homeless situation brought up. We don't think it'll be good for the kids. I'll leave you to check out the area and have some time to prepare as well. Someone should be coming down here a few minutes before we dismiss the students from their classrooms," she said as she turned around to head back to the office.

"Thank you!" I said as she continued walking.

I explored the cafeteria, picturing my audience for a while. Eventually, I got up onto the stage. I couldn't help but contemplate whether or not I should mention the homelessness. I wanted to serve the client as best as I could, but they weren't who I was there for. My mission was to reach and help the kids who may be facing similar struggles. This internal conflict kept on until about five minutes before my presentation. It was then that I made the conscious decision to tell my truth, homelessness and all, despite what the administration thought. As I told my story, I avoided making eye contact with members of the administration. I was either going to really piss them off or impress them. This added a whole new level of stress.

To my surprise, they absolutely loved the presentation after they saw how moved their students were.

Before I left, I thanked the principal for having me then headed out the door. John's son was sitting on a bench outside the building, waiting for me. We drove to their house—where I would be staying while I was in Eugene— and I was able to meet the rest of the family. Over dinner, John and I reviewed the next day. I would be speaking at the Hosea Homeless Drop-In Center, what I was most nervous for. After dinner, I excused myself and went straight to bed.

The next day, when it was time, John drove me over to the Drop-In Center. I hoped he wouldn't notice how tense I was. Speaking to homeless youth always made me a bit more nervous because it wasn't just my truth I was sharing, but it was theirs also. I could look into my audience and know for sure they were still in it, still in the homelessness.

"We announced that we're bringing dinner tonight. Pizza! So there should be a good turn out," John said, reassuring me. "We aren't sure how many will stay for the entire presentation, but we hope they all do."

I understood what he was trying to say and told him, "I don't expect them all to stay. I know the situation they're in. I'm no longer there, but they are, and I'll probably be hitting a lot of triggers."

Sure enough, when we arrived, there were about 45 homeless teenagers and young adults who showed up. No matter the size of the audience, I always give my all. So, once everyone was settled in, I began speaking, pouring my heart into my story just as I always did. Halfway through, more than half the audience had gotten up and walked out. By the time I finished, there were only about 15 teens left.

A young girl, with mismatched clothes, unkempt hair, who looked to be around 16, approached me crying. We sat down and I put my arm around her to try and comfort her. She leaned into my arm. We sat there until she was able to compose herself. We talked briefly before I asked, "If you don't mind me asking mija, what brought you to the streets?"

The look in her eyes told me she was about to share something painful. Her head dropped, and she started to share, "When I was little, my mom and I were so close. I thought she loved me… but what did I know, right? It seemed like we were fine, everything was great and then all of a sudden it wasn't."

I tried to make sense of what the young girl was saying. I could tell she was struggling to share her experience with me, to relive her trauma, so I stayed quiet and listened intently.

"I was stupid for thinking my mom cared about me… She would grab me and hold me down. She'd squeeze my wrists so hard my hands would go numb. Then she'd watch, she'd watch as her boyfriend molested me!" Tears were streaming down her face, "She didn't even flinch, she didn't change her mind halfway through. She let him finish and leave the room before she'd let me go. How? HOW? How could she do that to me?" She leaned harder into me, staining my shirt with her tears. "So I left. I finally left and ran to the streets. I've been on the streets ever since."

"Mija, I'm so sorry," I whispered, as I cried with her.

I wondered, *Will she ever wake up? Will she ever let go of the hurt her mother had caused her?* I gently moved her out of my arms to see her face.

"Mija, I'm going to tell you a quick story if you don't mind," I said.

She looked at me, waiting for me to begin.

"When I was 18 years old, just a little bit older than you, I decided to put myself in counseling. See, I was struggling with identity issues at the time and I felt like the only way I could get better was if I sought help. So one day, I attended a counseling session where there were about ten men of all ages and ethnicities. When I was sitting there, I started to feel weird because I noticed I was the youngest guy in the room, but even though I felt uncomfortable, I decided to stay. We started the session, and each man began disclosing information about his life and explaining why he was there. Out of all the ten men who spoke, one, in particular, stood out to me. He sat directly across from me and had peppered-grey hair. He must have been in his early 60s. He stood out to me because I connected to him the most, and it scared me."

"Wait, how did you connect with him?" she interrupted.

"I'm about to tell you right now," I said, then continued, "As the man introduced himself and began to tell his story, he started crying. I could see tears running down his face and at that moment his word became more real to me. He was talking about his father. He went on about how his father was mean to him as a child, how his father would abuse him, and that his father didn't love him. When I was listening to him, I saw myself in his story. I was asking myself the same questions he was. Why didn't my dad love me? Why did he do what he did? What did I do wrong to deserve what had happened to me at such a young age?"

Her eyes began to fill with tears again.

"Mija, that day I realized I didn't want to be the man who was sitting across from me. I didn't want to hold on to those questions for the rest of my life. They tell us that time heals all wounds, but how come over 50 years later his wounds weren't healed? He was over 60 years old and still living his life as the 12-year-old little boy who was hurt by his father. I didn't want that for me, and I certainly don't want that for you. We shouldn't wake up at 60 years old, ready to let go and start what life we have left. We can't be victims to someone else's actions forever."

I watched her as she wiped a few tears from her face. She composed herself before asking, "Do you blame me?"

I was taken back by her question. Of course I didn't blame her for what happened to her, but had I said something that might make her think otherwise? She must have read the look on my face because she restated her question.

"I mean, can you blame me for being here?" her tone of voice was more explicit. I knew what she was really asking me. She was asking if I was judging her. She wanted to know if I was judging her for running away, for being molested, for being homeless.

Reassuring her, I said, "I don't blame you. I can understand that life has taken so much from you already, but don't give it your future too. I know we may not be able to control what others do, but what we do have control over is how we respond. In life, we can either be a victim, survivor, or role model. We only get this life once, mija. Don't waste it. Don't live a life someone else has given you." She hugged me again, and I carried on, "Ask yourself mija, are you homeless because you want to be? Or is it because someone made you homeless? If the reason is that someone else made you homeless, then the next question you should ask yourself is; Am I in control of my life? If you're not in control, it's not your life. You have to make the right choices to live the life you want to live."

I took a moment to pause, I wanted to make sure she comprehended what I was saying. I continued, "Don't live your life as a victim, but I encourage you not to live your life as just a survivor either, take one more step. Be a role model."

Once we had both moved away from our heavy conversation, I tried to lighten the mood by complimenting her earrings. "Oh wow, look at your earrings. They look so different, where did you get them at?" I asked.

"These?" she said reaching for one, "I made them!"

"No way mija! That's awesome. How did you do that?"

"Well, I had a cat, his name was Romeo. But about a year ago, he died. So when he died, instead of burying him, I boiled him. These earrings are actually a part of his pelvis!" she said with pride, still holding one of the earrings in her hand.

I tried not to show my "what the hell" face, and stuttered, "That's... that's... very interesting... Well mija, I know you have to go. Thank you for sharing your story with me. I hope the things I shared with you tonight stick with you. Remember, never give up and NEVER give your future away to anyone or anything," I said as we hugged.

"Thank you Roy. You really made me want to do better for myself. Have a safe trip! Maybe you can come back some day!" she said as she walked over to the door.

I smiled back at her, waved goodbye, then sat down at the table where we spoke. I was horrified at what the young girl had just told me. *Was she mentally ill? Had she gone crazy due to her situation?* I thought about the type of mental state someone must be in to boil their cat, skin them, then take the bones to make earrings. A million questions and scenarios ran through my mind.

I couldn't help but wonder, who would this poor girl be if she had been given a fair chance at life? How broken was she and could she ever come out of it? When she ran to the streets, who knows what she did to medicate herself, to ease the pain she felt. Some people turn to sex, others to drugs, or whatever it is.

My wounds from being a homeless teenager turned me into a fractured young adult. I began using sex to feel loved, and it became an addiction. Every time I felt lonely or unloved, I could just have sex with someone, and I would feel okay for a few days. The pain of being unwanted was more significant than the disgust of being with a stranger. I was so broken on the inside that I allowed others to hurt me because I always knew they weren't hurting me more than I hurt myself. Deep down, I hated myself because there was something wrong with me. Something so wrong that nobody wanted me.

However, I was one of the lucky ones. I had mentors who came into my life and taught me to see my true value. It wasn't until I learned the difference between sex and love that I questioned; *How many people out there are walking around with an incurable STD or a child because all they wanted was to be loved?* I don't blame them because I know what it feels like to be hurt, alone, and unwanted. Oftentimes, an open conversation about sex is so taboo that we are left to figure it all out ourselves! I could only imagine how different my life would be if I didn't have the mentors who helped guide me to a healthier lifestyle.

This girl was me, without the mentors. My heart broke for her because I knew she didn't have the financial means to get the professional help she desperately needed. She had dug herself into a deep hole without even knowing it, and she might never live her life for herself. There's a good chance she'll be broken for the rest of her life, however long that is, because of the mental and physical pains placed on her. She was in such a horrible place in life that she would have to climb out of the hole that had been dug for her just to be at ground level with society.

## Life is Like the Side of a Cliff

One of my mentors, Dr. Sergeant, once said to me:

"When I think about life, I see it as a side of a cliff, and each person is born on different levels of this cliff. Some people are born near the top, so their climb up, where it's safe, may not be that long or hard. However, if they were to fall, more times than not, they would return to the spot in which they began…

"Others are born towards the middle of the cliff; these individuals must climb a little longer and harder. If they were to fall, more times than not, they too return to where they started, the middle of the cliff…

"Roy, when I think about your life, I'd say that you were born at the bottom of the cliff, but you've climbed longer and higher than most people will climb in their entire life. I caution you; If you fall, I don't know how far down you'll go."

My mentor shared that story with me when I began medicating myself with alcohol. He saw my destructive behavior, and his words opened my eyes. I did start at the bottom of the cliff, but despite how hard I worked, I didn't have a safety net to catch me. I've come to learn that my safety net is education. With every diploma, certificate, or degree you receive, you create a resting place on the side of this cliff we call life.

I was determined to climb as high as I could and leave my old world behind. I figured; If I could get myself to a level three in life, I could help the level twos and level ones. If I could climb even higher, and get to a level six in life, then I could help the level fives, fours, threes, twos and ones. But I asked myself, *What if I could get to a level TEN, at the top of the cliff?* I could help even more people who were still at level nine and below.

Every person is born at a different level, and we have to take the initiative to progress. It's up to us to reach new heights and create our own safety nets as we climb.

I reflected on our conversation for several minutes before I got up from the table where I was talking to the young girl and headed to the car. John was already waiting for me, so we could head back to his house in time for some dinner. I stayed quiet for most of the drive, still thinking about the girl's situation and all the others who might be in the same place. Encounters like these became constant reminders of why I was on tour.

# CHAPTER THIRTEEN

## Use Your Voice

WHEN WE ARRIVED at John's house, I enjoyed dinner with my host family and headed for bed. I was thankful the Crowder's allowed me to have my own room in their home. I needed time alone to reflect on the day. I laid in bed replaying the young girl's situation in my mind. Eventually, it brought back memories of my own.

***

A man I was close to had taken me in and allowed me to sleep in his spare bedroom. One night, right before bedtime, he said, "Roy, my cousin is coming into town and I'm going to have him sleep in your room." His comment puzzled me, I didn't understand why someone would be coming over so late. It was almost midnight. He then instructed me, "Tonight, you'll be sleeping in my room."

Those words frightened me, so I quickly asked, "If I'm sleeping in your room, then where are you gonna sleep?"

The man rebutted, "Well, I guess I'll just stay awake in the living room. Plus, it's late Roy. Why don't you go to bed?"

I got up from the couch and made my way to his room. I closed the door behind me, then reached for the knob in an attempt to lock it. I then realized that the door didn't even have a lock. I slowly climbed into his bed, covering myself with his blanket in the same way fear had covered my body. I laid in his dark room, watching the lights from the hallway flood in from under the door. Silently, I prayed, "God, please don't let him come in. God, please don't let him come in…"

That night, my prayers were answered, a shadow never appeared under the door. I was relieved but knew I wouldn't always be so lucky.

I woke up the next morning trying to convince myself I was overreacting and there was nothing to worry about. A few days passed, and everything seemed to be okay, so I didn't think much of the incident. Then early one evening, the man walked into the house holding a 44-ounce soda and said, "Hey Roy, I bought this for you at the corner store."

Excited that he thought about me, I said, "Wow, thanks!" He handed the soda to me, and I took a big slurp. I couldn't figure out the flavor, but it was sweet.

I was slowly sipping on it when he finally said, "Hurry up and drink it so we can go to dinner."

I wasn't sure why he was so concerned about me finishing the drink before we left. He usually let me take food and drinks in his car, but I didn't bother to question him about it this time. I chugged the drink, so he wouldn't be upset, and we made our way to the car.

As we drove closer to the restaurant, I began to feel weird. I struggled to keep my eyes open, and my head started dropping. We pulled into the parking lot of Capparelli's on Main, near downtown San Antonio, and he parked the car. I waited for him to switch off the ignition, so we could get out, but he didn't. We sat there in awkward silence as I fought against my body wanting to pass out.

After about five minutes I asked, "So, are we gonna get out?"

"Oh, yeah, yeah. Let's get out," he said as he finally turned off the car.

We walked into the front door of the restaurant, and in the distance, I heard my name being called. I looked around and saw a familiar face. It was a lady I had met—through the man I was with—that I had grown close to. Her soft brown eyes had never stood out to me as much as they did that night. I think it was because I saw her as my saving grace. Even though she was half his size, I felt a sense of comfort having her there. As she leaned in to hug me,

I wrapped my arms around her tightly and whispered with fear, "Please don't leave me. Please. Don't leave me."

Slowly, we unlocked from our embrace. She was now staring at me with concern, and I was scared her expression would alarm him. I stared back at her, subtly shaking my head, my eyes begging her not to give me away.

Finally, she asked in a cheerful voice, "Are you guys just getting here?"

I replied, "Yes ma'am."

"Great, can I join you?" she asked.

Before the man could reply, I quickly said, "Yes! Please, please join us."

The waitress walked us to our table, and as we sat down, the man leaned over and whispered, "Get whatever you want."

At first, I thought he was talking about alcohol because on several occasions he would order shots and slip them to me when no one was watching. Being 15 years old, I thought it cool, but looking back now, I am sure it was a part of his plan.

I responded quickly, "Coffee, I'll take coffee!"

He was a little taken back, "That's all you want? Only coffee?"

It was then that I realized he wasn't referring to alcohol when he said I could order whatever I wanted. He meant I could order whatever food I wanted to eat. The evening naturally progressed, and everything seemed normal again. At one point, he got up and went to the bathroom. As soon as he was out of sight, the lady looked at me and asked, "Roy, is everything okay?"

I looked down at the floor because I wasn't sure if I was overreacting.

"Yes ma'am, I'm sorry. I just didn't feel good," I replied, a bit embarrassed.

"Roy is there anything you want to tell me? Are you safe?"

"Yes ma'am," I said, lightening my tone, "it's nothing like that."

I was lying but I didn't want to cause a scene, nor was I sure about what was really going on.

Several minutes later he rejoined us at the table and I tried to behave as normal as possible. I was so confused as I sat there thinking to myself, *Why are you overreacting?*

In the days that followed, I couldn't get those two incidents out of my mind.

I still felt uncomfortable and wanted to leave but didn't know how I would escape. I started packing all of my things into my bag when I had a moment of clarity. It was like being punched in the stomach, and I fell on the bed crying. I realized I wasn't overreacting, and that wasn't the first time it had happened. Running through my mind was a third incident I couldn't explain, until that day.

I remembered one morning, waking up in the man's guest bedroom but struggling to remember how I got there. I didn't remember walking into his house or going to bed the night before. I sat up in bed confused, and instantly felt a burning sensation below that hurt. My walk to the bathroom was more of a waddle because I was so uncomfortable. I grabbed a mirror to examine myself and noticed I was ripped, and bleeding. To ease the pain, I applied Vaseline. Clueless and embarrassed about what had happened at that moment, I didn't tell anyone.

It all made sense now, it wasn't the first time he drugged me, he had done it before. I had been raped.

***

As I laid there in John's spare bedroom, still staring at the light coming from under the door, I wept. I wept for myself, for the girl I had just met, and the thousands of youth who fall victim to sexual abuse. It is never okay for anyone to put their hands on you! Which is why—each time I share my story with students—I tell them, "It is never okay for anyone to touch you, and if you find yourself in that type of situation, say something. If you're scared to say something, write a note for your teacher, principal, counselor, or anyone you trust, to find."

I don't know how I fell asleep that night, but when I woke up, I thanked God for allowing me another day to try and make a difference.

## Lake Mills, Iowa - 13 Months into the Tour

As I began the second year on the road, I started to ask myself, "What am I learning on this tour?" I had seen so much, reflected during the long drives, and learned from so many amazing leaders across the country.

Phase three of the tour was a week away, and my nerves were starting to build again. I knew the challenges that lie ahead. Perhaps if I had someone traveling with me again, the burden wouldn't be so heavy. As I spoke with people about the tour, many of them gave me a similar response, "It must be amazing to travel so much!" I would have to agree with them; It's incredible to travel. But, it's far from glamorous. Although it's a life-changing opportunity, it comes at a price.

During the previous phase of the tour, I spent a lot of time alone, driving from city to city. I was able to reflect on my past, present, and future. I understood where I had come from, my homeless experience, but that wasn't me anymore. I needed to stop focusing on the old Roy. I had come so far, now I just needed to plan where I wanted to go in life. What were my new goals?

It was in the middle of the night, on one of those long and lonely drives, that I came to a conclusion, *This depression stems from my presentations.* Every time I stepped before an audience, I had to relive the horror that tore my family apart. Speaking almost every day, at least 4 - 5 times a week, I was digging up all the hardships of my past. I was beyond burnt out, the tour had consumed me. The crazy thing was, I chose to relive it! I thought that my story could inspire hope in others.

However, I needed to figure out a way to battle against my depression and not let it consume me. If I didn't, there wouldn't have been a tour, and I wouldn't be helping anyone. I knew I wasn't alone, but emotionally I felt like I was. I was trying to be a role model and a national leader, but often I wondered, *Who I could turn to for hope? Who motivates the motivator?* I was scared that if I spoke about my depression people would look at me as a weak leader. I needed an outlet.

I had already been sharing my journey of the tour with my followers on Facebook, but now my posts became more like venting sessions. I was reluctant to share my raw emotions but figured it could be a win-win situation if I worded my posts correctly. I set an example for the students, that talking about your feelings is okay, and it would also be the outlet I was looking for. This was helpful until one afternoon I received a message from an acquaintance, who will go unnamed. In the message, he encouraged me not to share my personal emotions of feeling alone and defeated. He thought it wasn't right for my public image or a good example for the young people who looked up to me. I had mixed emotions about his response. I certainly didn't want to set a bad example for the students, but I also didn't want to give them a false sense of reality.

I wanted the students to understand that life isn't the same as what is often portrayed on social media. We can't put a filter on our problems to make them better. If we want a better life, we have to deal with the issues. Many of us have asked the questions; Can I really do this? Will I make it? These thoughts are prevalent in our culture. Why? Because life isn't easy.

However, one of the greatest lessons I've learned during my experience on the tour is this: In life, we need each other. Our dreams, motivation, and success are tied to those we surround ourselves with. The key is to find people who believe in you, have a positive outlook on life, and want to see you succeed even if your success outweighs theirs.

Now, here's some street wisdom for you. Although we need each other, never get to the point that you are entirely dependent on anyone else. You should be able to walk or crawl on your own. Your support group is only there to make sure you don't give up and help you open doors of opportunity.

## Can I Come to Hear You Speak?

One evening, when I was scrolling through Facebook on my phone in a cafe, I received a message.

"Hello sir, my name is Jose Celis," the Facebook message read. "I saw you speak several months ago at a United States Hispanic Leadership Institute Regional Conference and have been following your work ever since. I noticed you were coming to Chicago on your tour. I was wondering, can I come to hear you speak again?"

I responded, "Hey Mijo, thank you for writing to me. Yes, I will be coming to Chicago on the Homeless by Choice tour. You're more than welcome to come to any of my events!"

"Great! Where are you speaking?"

"That's my problem. Currently, I don't have any speaking engagements lined up. I haven't been able to find anyone who will let me speak in your area."

"What? Seriously? Sir, if you don't mind, can I help you find places to speak?" he wrote back.

I knew he was young, but I thought it couldn't hurt. Any help I could get would be fantastic, so we exchanged contact information.

About a week later I heard from Jose. This time, he called me.

"Hey sir, it's Jose from Chicago," he said.

"Hi mijo, great to hear from you. What's going on?"

"I just want to let you know, I found six places for you to speak! I was able to get you into two colleges, a middle school, a high school and two community events," he said with pride.

This news took me by surprise, "Seriously mijo? Oh my God, thank you!"

I actually had a lot of presentations in Chicago because I was able to connect with Chicago International Charter School. They were actually a Godsend, because they got me a hotel in downtown Chicago for five nights, my entire time there.

My first presentation was at CICS-Longwood with Principal Auffant, a passionate leader. As we walked his halls, I was impressed by how he knew every student's name and their story. The students seemed to really take to him as well, he was youthful, well dressed, and personable. My presentation at Longwood was a great start to my time in Chicago.

Every night I returned to the hotel, I focused on emailing schools east of Chicago because I didn't have a single event booked. By the third night, I had emailed thousands of principals, counselors, parent liaisons, and teachers but not a single person replied. I wasn't sure what I was going to do because my last scheduled presentation was the next day and I had nowhere to go after that.

It was the time for my last presentation, one that was organized by Jose. I was scheduled to speak in Boystown, an LGBTQ+ area of Chicago, at an old church converted into a homeless shelter. As I waited for people to arrive, in walked a slender young man with dark hair. He wore a huge smile, and in his hand, he held a copy of the book, *Chicken Soup for Soul: Extraordinary Teens*. I recognized it because my life story is summarized in that book. I thought, *That has to be Jose.*

He walked up to me and started to say, "Hi I'm—"

"Jose, right?" I interrupted.

He laughed, "Yes sir, I'm Jose."

"What you got there?" I asked, pointing to the book.

A little embarrassed he replied, "I bought it, hoping you would sign it for me."

"Of course, I'd love to sign it for you! Do you have a pen?"

He pulled out a black sharpie and handed it to me. As I was signing his book, he said, "I'd like for you to meet my mom."

I looked up and greeted her, "Hi, it's nice to meet you. You have a wonderful son."

Just as I was about to continue signing the book, he said, "I'd also like you to meet…"

I looked up and over his shoulder. A line of people stood behind him. I laughed inside as he introduced me to his girlfriend, mother, sister, mother's best friend, and brother.

After signing his book, they all sat down and waited for my presentation to start. The room didn't fill up, but I wasn't expecting it to. I knew I was at a homeless teen drop-in center. No one could have shown up that day except for Jose and the group of people he brought, and I would have been happy with it.

Since that day, Jose and I have developed a close friendship. He's even introduced me to his cousins and friends, who I now call my Chicago family; Laura, Mireya, Lily, Ryan, Sergio, and Julio! We always try to get together for dinner when I'm in town.

## A Storm is Approaching

I made it back to my hotel and started packing up my bags. I still didn't know where I was going to go or where I would speak, but I knew I would figure it out. Even if I had to go to every school on my route and personally talk to the principals, I would.

I grabbed the remote control and put on CNN to catch up on current events. While I was packing, I heard a breaking news alert that Chicago was preparing for a blizzard that was due to hit the next day. I stopped folding up my pants and sat on the edge of my hotel bed watching the news intently. There was no way I could get caught in a blizzard. I didn't have the money to rent a hotel for myself and—being from Texas—there was no way I was going to drive on ice-covered roads.

I thought to myself, *Maybe the Big Man upstairs is looking out for me, again.* I had been stuck in a city before, when my sister Tammy was on tour with me and we were in Houston, Texas. The only difference this time was I didn't have a place to stay. When I was in Houston, Art and Virgie Ornelas had taken us in for what they thought was only going to be 3 nights. We ended up staying with them for two weeks because the tour ran out of money. Virgie and her friends became like our family. As a collective, they supported and housed us.

One day it was Marcos Rubalcava and his wife Erika feeding us, the next day it was Shelley Zendejas or Vernon Williams. Shelley and Vernon were so good to me on the tour, they donated every paycheck for months! But sadly, I wasn't in Houston, I didn't have my Houston family to save me. I was in Chicago and a storm was approaching.

I got up from the edge of the bed and rushed to pack the rest of my things. My mind was racing, trying to figure out what I was going to do before the storm hit at 10:00 am the next morning. I knew I had made a mistake designing the tour route in the Northern part of the country during the winter months. As I finished packing, I set my hotel alarm for 3:00 am. My plan was to leave Chicago and drive straight for Miami, Florida in hopes that I wouldn't be caught in the middle of the blizzard.

Thankfully, I heard the alarm go off and swiftly made my way downstairs to load all my bags into the tour car.

The bellman questioned me, "Are you sure you want to leave? It's going to get bad out there."

"I heard! I'm gonna try and beat the storm before it hits."

He looked at me like I was crazy, "Well, good luck then. Be safe out there."

I thanked him as I jumped into the driver's seat and hit the road.

Chicago looked like a ghost town. There wasn't a single car on the road. I began to question my decision to leave, but I knew I couldn't stay. On only 4 hours of sleep, I drove through the night and made it as far as Atlanta, Georgia before I pulled over to rest. By the next day, I made it to South Beach, Florida. I dug my feet into the sand in 70-degree heat and looked over at the glistening sea. I was literally a beach bum!

Still with nowhere to go, I googled *Chicago Blizzard,* to see if I had made the right choice by leaving. Not far into my search, I saw *The New York Times* posted an article, entitled, "Chicago Humbled by Powerful Storm." Drivers were stranded on Lake Shore Drive, the same road I was on when I left the area. The following day it was reported they received over 21 inches of snow and 7 deaths were related to the storm.

Since I didn't have any presentations lined up at the time, I figured I would reroute the tour and try to secure presentations from Miami to New York. I really do think God was watching over me during that crucial decision for the tour because once I started emailing schools for the new tour route, I was getting responses and securing dates.

## Baby Ray Helps the Tour

It was in Chicago that I received a random text message from Baby Ray. I didn't bother to pay much attention to it, mostly because I had so many presentations and a storm to outrun! When I was finally able (and remembered) to get back to his message, it read:

"Hey big bro, I just wanted you to know that I deposited $70 into your bank account."

I was grateful for what he did but wasn't sure where he was getting his money from. I went to check my bank account and sure enough, there was $70 deposited! Then I noticed, just two days before his text, he had deposited $80 into my account. *Had he gotten a job I didn't know about?*

A few days later, during a phone call with my mom, I asked, "Mom, did Baby Ray get a job?"

"No mijo. Why?" she asked with concern.

"He's been sending me money, and I'm just curious where he's getting it from. But don't worry about it mom, I'll ask him about it."

It wasn't a huge concern of mine at the time, so I didn't bother to ask him about it right away. Several days had passed since the phone call with my mom when I received another text from Baby Ray that read, "Hey bro, I just deposited another $65."

My attention was now caught. Something didn't seem right to me, so I called him to make sure he wasn't stealing or selling drugs for money. When he answered, I got straight to the point.

"Ray, where are you getting this money?" I asked.

"Well, I know you need money for your tour, so I made bracelets that say Never Give Up, and I've been selling them to my friends at school," he replied.

I couldn't believe it. I was so proud of my little brother for thinking up a solution like that.

"Are you serious mijo? That's amazing! Do you think I can bring those bracelets with me on tour?"

"Yeah, for sure. I'll send you some, but you have to make me the marketing manager of the tour," he demanded.

I laughed and agreed, "Okay Baby Ray, you're officially the Homeless by Choice tour marketing manager!"

My teenage brother may have helped me lighten some of the heavy load on tour, but it wouldn't be enough.

# CHAPTER FOURTEEN

## I'll Give You My Best

### Raleigh, North Carolina - 15 Months into the Tour

THERE WAS SO much going on in my mind and heart! I felt as though my emotions were constantly alternating between elated and despondent. I had come so far in life, there seemed to be no reason for me to be feeling negative emotions, but I was. I just couldn't seem to shake it. I know it may not be easy to understand, and some may say, "Roy just get over it!" and I wish I could, but it's not that easy. Where are these emotions coming from? Were they birthed from years of a fractured childhood?

A part of me felt unaccomplished.

On Facebook, in a casual conversation with a student, I even mentioned how I felt like giving up. He replied, "Please don't give up! I need to know there are real heroes out there!" After reading his response on the screen, I hated myself for even considering the thought.

I wondered, how do I fill this emptiness?

As humans, we try to fill it with many different things. Some with love and companionship, others with alcohol, drugs, or sex, and some choose a more spiritual path... God.

Each one of these paths comes with their own set of challenges. I know, I have lived many of them. Life is such an emotional roller-coaster! It's great if you're an adrenaline junkie, I guess. But what about the person who decides they don't like the ride and wants to get off early? While this is an excruciating thought, especially for the family and friends of that person, I don't judge them. I may not understand their decision, but what I do understand is their pain.

There have been nights where I've laid in bed and cried my eyes out, asking, *WHY GOD, WHY?!* With no answer that I could hear or feel, it made it hard for me to believe that things would get better. I guess that's the whole purpose of faith. I don't blame God, nor do I despise him. It's just hard to live a life with so many struggles, and always choose to learn from them to better myself.

I've heard it said that there is nothing new under the sun, but I'm not the sun, I'm me. All these experiences are new to me, must be learned by me, and must be overcome by me. Even if I didn't sign up to learn these lessons, it doesn't matter, that's life and life isn't fair. I think once we learn to accept that, it's easier to roll with the punches. I just wonder, *How many lessons must I learn to finally be happy? Will I ever be satisfied?*

I know that happiness comes in so many different forms, which is beautiful, but what does *my* happiness look like? If the average life expectancy is 77.6 years, I have a few years left to figure that out. Maybe that is what I am doing on this tour.

Identifying that which makes you happy is the journey. I know for a fact that music ministers to my soul. It heightens whatever emotion I am feeling. But Pizza makes me happy too. Now that I am an adult, paying my bills on time also makes me really happy! I can't help but think we are all the same, we share this giant rock we call Earth and spend our lives searching for our happiness.

## Having the Right People in Your Corner

I had just finished speaking at Heritage High School in Wake Forest, North Carolina. Although the presentation went well, I couldn't get away from the black cloud that hung over me. For the past several weeks, I had been through an emotional hurricane. My car kept breaking down, I wasn't sleeping enough, and I was reliving my traumatic past over and over. I could feel myself spiraling further into depression each time I presented. I felt done. Loneliness encompassed me even in the company of others.

My host families would ask, "Are you alright Roy? You must be exhausted."

It was as if they could see through the facade, through my fake smile.

I would reply, "Oh yeah, I'm great. Just tired from traveling."

I knew it wasn't the whole truth. I knew I needed a break from the tour, I needed to get away and be alone to recharge. If not, I wasn't going to make it.

As I sat in my car, I reviewed my calendar looking for a few days I could take off and get away from it all. I spotted a few empty days in a row. I decided to block them out as personal time because I didn't want to accidentally agree to speak on those days. I was experiencing major internal conflict. One part of me said, *Screw it, quit the tou*r, but then I would read through the messages students would send me and the other part of me would say, *Keep on fighting, Roy!*

I knew I had to make up my mind one way or the other, and I was going to use my break to decide.

I booked a trip to Dallas, Texas from March 19th - March 23rd. Thankfully, a friend of mine, Riley Nail, was able to get me a room at his hotel, the ZaZa. As soon as I had everything lined up, I texted James and told him I was coming into town. James was, and still is, my ride-or-die. I know I could have stayed with him in Dallas, but I needed some alone time. He didn't question me when I suggested he come to visit me at the hotel versus me stopping by his house. He promised that he'd see me under any circumstances when I arrived.

Sure enough, the second day into my break, James texted me asking for my room number. I sent it to him, and moments later he was knocking at my door. I opened the door and greeted him with a forced smile and turned away to walk back to my bed. The room was dark and cold. I had the blinds shut, the only light in the room radiated from the television screen. I sat back on the edge of the bed to watch the news. I was still feeling depressed and emotionally drained, but it was great to see my best friend, even though I wasn't showing it. I wasn't my normal, high energy self, and James noticed. I was giving him a bunch of half-smiles and snappier retorts to his questions, but he knew me well. We caught up for a few minutes before he said it, "What's going on with you Roy? This isn't you. I've never seen you look so… depressed."

He paused for a moment, then continued and finally asked the question I had been dreading; "What are you even doing in Dallas anyway? Shouldn't you be on tour?"

I sighed, and there was a long pause before I responded.

"I'm quitting."

"What?"

"I'm quitting the tour," I couldn't believe I finally verbalized it. It hurt even more to say it to someone else, rather than to just saying it to myself.

"What?! Roy, what are you talking about? You're kidding with me, right?" He would have kept spitting out questions if I hadn't cut him off.

"No man, I'm serious. I can't do this anymore. It's way too much for me now. I'm overwhelmed, tired, I'm depressed all th—"

"But what about all those kids? You can't quit on them! You can't," he interrupted.

"James you just don't get it. You don't know how hard this is. Last time you came on tour with me, you only lasted two weeks! Remember? Imagine being on the road for the past 18 months!"

I didn't mean to call him out, but I was frustrated and wanted him to see things from my perspective. Deep down, I was hoping he would tell me it was okay to quit.

I kept trying to explain myself, "I can't do it by myself anymore. It's tough man… It's taking so much out of me."

Again, there was another long silence between us.

"Well Roy, I'm sorry… I'm sorry for quitting on you last time, but I'm not letting *you* quit. You've come this far, and it doesn't matter how tired you are, you're not quitting," James took a deep breath.

He looked side to side a couple of times, rubbing his head and gritting his teeth. I had no idea why he looked so troubled.

He finally looked back at me, took another deep breath, and said, "I'm going on tour with you… again."

"What?" I couldn't believe what he said.

"Well, you just said you can't do it by yourself anymore. If I go with you, you won't be by yourself, so there's no excuse for you not to finish the tour. I'm gonna help you," his voice was stern.

I was still in disbelief, "James are you serious right now? Swear?"

"Yeah man! But I'm telling you right now, if I come with you, we're finishing your tour. I'm not gonna leave what I have just for you to quit on me," he laughed, "We got this Roy. I swear I'll last longer than two weeks."

"Oh yeah? Ha! Man, of course I'm not gonna quit if I have you with me. I just need someone to help me along the way."

I went from feeling depressed to excited. I didn't want to quit the tour. I don't think anybody ever wants to just "quit" something they've poured their heart into. It was too much for me, and I didn't want to sacrifice my mental health to continue.

He said, "I guess I'll be 'homeless by your choice,' again."

We both laughed.

As we talked more throughout the night, we came up with a solid plan. He would move out, put his two weeks in at work, and I'd pay for his flight to wherever I was once he was ready to come.

He ended up meeting me at Shenandoah Valley Regional Airport in Virginia on Easter Sunday. We spent the holiday with my friend, Principal Theresa Davis, in Grottoes, Virginia. I met her when I spoke at her school inside a juvenile center, and I don't think I've met a kinder person in my life. Theresa has a huge heart and lets me stay with her anytime I'm in the area. She even gave me a spare key, just in case.

Once it was time to work, James' job became driving me as we moved from city to city. Because he freed me from driving, I was able to email clients, which saved me so much time because it usually took around several hundred emails just to get a response or two. An unofficial job he took on was carrying the conversation every time we stayed at a new home. By the end of the day, I was often so drained from speaking, writing emails, and talking with students, that when we arrived at our host family, I was too tired to carry hour long conversations. I had nothing left to give. As soon as we'd walk through the door, James would start asking the host family questions to start a conversation. He would ask about their careers, the town, their family, anything he could think of, so I could rest mentally.

The work James was doing for me wasn't a paid position. I didn't pay him anything directly, but I was able to pay his bills. Not always on time, but I paid for them. Knowing this, he still stayed with me until I finished the tour and didn't make any money. Again, he is my ride or die! He sacrificed his relationship, his job, and his living situation because he believed in my dream.

These are the type of friends you want in your corner. The ones who don't let you give up and help you chase your dreams. Having the right support system in your corner is vital to success.

## How Did you Do It?

I was invited by Ms. Whitney Carnes to address the students at Pickens County Mountain Charter Night School in Jasper, Georgia. During the question and answer session, one student asked, "How did you do it?"

I was a little confused.

"How did I do what?" I replied.

"How did you learn to be better and not bitter?"

I hadn't really thought about it, but I told a story of how I redesigned my thoughts.

"The true character of a man will be shown during times of tribulation rather than times of peace. Most times, my tribulation consumed me. Why? Because I did have a core set of values."

I looked around the room and noticed a wave of confusion spread across the student's faces.

I explained, "While moments in life were tough and I made some bad decisions, it was those lessons I learned growing up that kept me from being destroyed. Even though my parents left me, they still played a huge role in helping me become the person I am today."

I focused my attention solely on the young lady who asked the question, "You see, we learn lessons through the good and the bad. I'm incredibly flawed, but I don't allow those flaws to keep me from chasing my passions and I'm passionate about helping others. I acknowledge my shortcomings but use them to become the best man I can be."

I reexamined the room and noticed a few students nodding their heads. With a deep breath, I continued.

"In life, we learn many lessons. Some lessons will come from books or teachers, and some, from personal experiences. We must learn to identify the positive lessons and hold on to them. But how can we figure out which lessons those are?"

I inhaled deeply, then shared with the students, "Speaking merely from my personal experience, here was my method: I analyzed my life. With a sheet of paper and pen in hand, I asked myself, 'Who do I want to be? How do I want to be remembered?'," I paused for a moment to allow the students to reflect on my questions.

"As I've learned from my mentor, we must not only leave a legacy, we must also live a legacy. I sat at my dining room table and made a list of everything I hated about myself. I then made a second list directly next to it, writing the opposite meaning of the negative words. The first one read, stupid. Next to it I wrote, brilliant!"

I scanned the room to be sure they were following what I was saying before I continued, "I wrote the word "brilliant" because that was the word my mentor used. She would look at me, and say, 'Roy. You. Are. Brilliant.' I didn't believe her because I felt stupid, but I hated feeling that way. I knew I didn't have a good education because I was never in school. My writing was horrible, and I couldn't spell. I hated it."

The students looked at me surprised as if they didn't realize that I, too, could have insecurities.

I continued with the second one, "Next I wrote, I am attractive. I had always felt that I wasn't good enough and had a stupid idea that if I were better looking, someone would love me."

As I spoke, I remembered why I had even started to think about this.

When I was younger, every time I had to leave a host family, or I was abandoned by a loved one, I asked myself, *What's wrong with me? Why don't they love me?* Subconsciously, I had learned to accept the idea that I wasn't good enough, attractive enough, or smart enough. Now I know that is far from the truth, but this shows how at moments in our life we can learn lessons and never even know it.

"Number three on my list; I will be a good son, brother, and friend. My family has always been important to me, but we were all so fractured at one point. Each one of us was dealing with our demons and trying to figure out what to do with our childhood pain. For this reason, I continue to work on my relationship with my siblings."

I wiped my brow and continued, "For example, I remember one day, I was sitting at the kitchen table with my sisters when I suggested we all go around and list our strengths and weaknesses. I had just learned about S.W.O.T. (strengths, weakness, opportunities, and threats) in my business class at HSU, and I wanted to apply the same concept to my family. My sisters were willing to participate, and we shared—with love—our views of each other. Our goal was to help each other become better people."

I noticed some of the students engaging with me even more intently as if it were a list they were thinking about writing themselves. "Number four, I will hug more and smile more. This one is tough for me to share and I'm going to change the people's names due to the sensitivity of the story, and out of respect for the family," I told them.

"I received a call from my mother one day asking me if I remembered a girl named Heather from our church. I knew who she was talking about but didn't understand why she was bringing her up. Then, she said, 'Well Roy, Heather's no longer with us' hearing those words shocked me."

I gulped before continuing.

"I asked my mother, 'What happened?' I came to learn that Heather took her own life. She had gotten into a fight with her boyfriend and, later that day, after having dinner with her family, she excused herself to her room. That's when her parents heard the gunshot. She left a letter for her family saying, 'I am so sorry I'm not strong enough. Please, hug more and smile more!'"

Her words broke my heart. There is no reason why anyone should have to say, "hug more and smile more." Those actions don't cost us anything. We have to be better people, care for each other, and be there for each other. I learned from that advice, and now, I always try to hug and smile as much as possible.

As I finished sharing, I noticed a young man get up and walk out of the room with tears in his eyes. Following right behind him was the school counselor, which reassured me that he was in the right hands.

"Number five, I will be a good person. After I wrote this down, I really had to define what it meant to me. I figured I could be good to people who are good to me, but that's easy. To be a good person, I'd have to be good to those that weren't good to me. This one wasn't easy to learn and is probably the one I have to remind myself of the most."

"For number six, I wrote that I would focus on the good in others," I said, pointing to the students in the room. "After all the psychology classes I took, I've come to learn that we're all broken in some way. This understanding helped me develop the compassion to forgive my parents. I learned I had to separate a person from their brokenness, love them, and try to help them. Now, when I see others, I look past their brokenness and try to see the good in them."

"Number seven, I will chase my dreams. I felt like God gave me a second chance at life, and I wasn't going to waste it. There's a band called *Five for Fighting*, and they have a song called, 'Chances.' The first verse of that song always gets me emotional because there's so much truth in it. The line is, 'chances are when said and done, who will be the lucky ones to make it all the way?' I felt I was one of the lucky ones and, because of that, I wasn't going to waste my life by not chasing my dreams."

What many people don't know, is there was one more number on my list, number 8. While working in schools, I usually stop at number seven because the next one is about my faith. Some may say I shouldn't be embarrassed about sharing my faith, but I'm not. I just believe in showing it through actions because words are cheap. There is a time and place for everything.

Number eight on my list is, I love God and seek to make Him happy.

Growing up, I loved going to church. I became a youth pastor for the first time at the age of 12. During that time, our youth group had 15 - 20 kids ranging from 11 - 18 years old.

Eventually, I stopped going to church because I felt like I was seen as the "bad kid" and the church leader's kids were seen as perfect, which I knew wasn't the case. Maybe it was because I asked too many questions. I remember this one time I attended a vacation bible school and we had a guest speaker. He was talking to us about how to dress when we came to church.

He said, "Girls, you shouldn't wear short skirts to church because you are going to cause men to look and the bible says in Romans 14:13, 'never put a stumbling block or hindrance in the way of a brother.'"

I was confused by his statement, so I raised my hand and said, "I don't get it, why can't a girl wear a skirt if she wants to? What if that's all she has? Plus, is it really her that has the problem, or the man with the lust in his eye?"

After I said it, the kids around me started laughing, and I think it pissed the man off. He took my comment as though I was combative, even though I wasn't. I didn't understand why he was trying to justify a man's actions by blaming it on a girl. Each person should be responsible for their own actions. I'm sure he viewed me as a troublesome kid like everyone else. Either way, things were just getting worse at home, so I just stopped going to church. Even though I left the church, my faith has never left me, and I still wanted to make sure I made God smile.

Now, let me be clear, I am no longer twelve years old and have lived the life of twelve men. I don't know why the Big Man upstairs loves me because I am far from being His best kid, but I thank Him for always being there for me and having my back. It might not be when I want it, but it's always right on time. Sometimes I wish He would show up earlier though.

When I finally brought my presentation to a close, I realized I had kept the students a little longer than I was supposed to. They didn't seem to mind though, as I was thanked with a lot of handshakes and hugs.

As I was packing up my laptop, I noticed two young men hanging around. They caught my attention because before the event started, they walked up to me and said angrily, "We don't wanna be here, but the counselors are making us come, so you better be good!"

I had replied, "I'll give you the best I have."

During the presentation, I avoided looking at them because I didn't want them to feel that I was talking directly at them or challenging them. After standing there for a while, sizing me up, they finally approached me.

"Hey sir, we're sorry about how we were acting earlier when we first walked in."

"It's not a problem, I take it you enjoyed the presentation?"

"Yeah sir, it was good," said the taller of the two. He continued, "My name's Brandon, by the way, do you think we could do the honor of carrying your bags to your car?"

I smiled and agreed.

On our way to my car, they began sharing their life stories with me. I gladly listened and gave advice when they asked. I could have written those two young men off as rude or troubled, but because I was willing to show them my brokenness, I'm still friends with Brandon today!

# CHAPTER FIFTEEN

## Who am I?

### Philadelphia, Pennsylvania - 19 Months into the Tour

IT WAS A day I dreamt about for years. I never knew if it would come to pass, but it was always just that—a dream of mine. This was one of the moments in my life that would mean everything. This dream was about to come true, and I was extremely nervous.

When I received the call to be the keynote speaker at the FEW Conference, I reached out to my mentor immediately.

"Mrs. K, you are never gonna guess who asked me to come speak!" I exclaimed.

"Who mijo, who?" she inquired.

"FEW, the organization you were speaking at when I snuck in for the free meal!"

"Oh, God is good! Where will the conference be?"

"It'll be in Philadelphia, sometime in July."

"Find out what day for me!"

"Oh, right! Let me check," I put her on hold briefly as I looked for the date. "The 17th! It'll be on July 17th in Philadelphia."

"Roy, you're not going to believe it. I'm speaking at a conference in Philadelphia on July 16th!" She continued with excitement, "Mijo, I'll change my flight! This time, I'll sit in the audience as *you* speak and maybe I can steal a meal from you!"

After further investigation, we learned that Mrs. K's conference was right across the street from the hotel I would be speaking in. The morning of my presentation, I walked across the street and waited in the lobby for her to come down. She was dressed to the nines. We linked arms as I escorted her across the street to my event.

My stomach was doing somersaults. After all, there was going to be about 1,500 people in the audience and my mentor would be sitting in the front row.

This presentation wasn't like all the others. Yes, I wanted to inspire the audience, but this was personal. It was going to be the pinnacle of my journey at that point. I had a chance to relive a moment in my past, but this time, with a happy ending.

This was the same conference that I had snuck into as a homeless teenager. The last time I was here, my heart was pounding in my chest like a blacksmith's hammer. I was feeling a similar physical sensation but—this time—it was from disbelief that I had made it this far.

As I sat there waiting to take the stage, so many thoughts were going through my mind. How did I get to this point? What should I say? What if I forget to thank Joyce Hageman or Sue Webster?

Under my breath, I said to myself, "Roy you can't forget to thank Sue, don't forget Sue! She is the president of the organization."

My mentor, who was sitting next to me, could sense how nervous I was. She reached over and put her hand on top of mine and said, "You are going to be great mijo, just say what's in your heart."

I gave her a weak smile, and in a shaky voice I said, "I'm just so nervous."

As the audience was eating their meal, I could barely bring myself to touch my plate. I was lost in my thoughts when, in a faint voice, I heard Ms. Webster introducing me. My hands left a small wet patch against my bouncing knees. As I stood up, I wiped it off on the side of my neatly pressed suit. I could see the audience clapping, but I couldn't hear them. It was an eerie feeling, as though I was in a twilight zone. There was no turning back now. I walked cautiously to the edge of the stage, which was about 10 yards away. The walk felt eternal, and I swear my body moved in slow motion. I made my way up the east ramp. Waiting for me at center stage, with a huge smile, was Mrs. Sue Webster, president-elect of the Federal Employed Women's Conference.

Mrs. Webster was wearing a flamingo pink and black pantsuit that matched my tie. Her hair was auburn and styled into a pixie cut. Her hazel eyes glistened with warmth as she stood there, her arms extended towards me. I found a sense of comfort in her embrace and, for a moment, I stopped thinking. I thanked her, and as soon as she handed me the microphone my mind spun into chaos again. My heart was thumping even louder. I swear the audience could see it through my suit. I glanced at the sea of faces. Either they were expectant, or extremely kind. I took a deep breath through my nose. *Come on, Roy.* I approached the podium.

I glanced over to the far-left corner towards the back of the banquet hall. Fourteen years ago, I was there. My life changed that day, and now I'm on the other side. I could see my 16 year-old-self watching me with dubious eyes, but mainly just tucking into a free meal.

It was like the Christmas story, where the old man is visited by the three ghosts; the Ghost of Christmas Past, Ghost of Christmas Present, and Ghost of Christmas Yet to Come. Scrooge is the character's name. I felt just like Ebenezer Scrooge, and I too was being visited by my past.

I was more focused on the servers placing the dinner plates in front of each guest. I saw myself waiting, anticipating my turn. I would have loved to run over and talk to my younger self.

I want to tell him; "Little do you know what your future will hold. All the fears and struggles you're currently facing will be used to help thousands of youth throughout the world."

His light pale skin, sunken eyes, and mismatched clothes made it obvious he didn't belong in the room. Why did no one say anything? Did they know that he needed to be there? The guests greeted him with warm eyes and the same smile they used to welcome everyone else.

Finally, his meal arrived, and I could see his eyes light up, like the moment a match strikes the matchbox. Still carrying the values once taught to him, he thanked the server for the meal. Not knowing which one to grab, he reaches for the fork closest to him. Even though I can see him, he can't see me. How badly I want to tell him that it will all be alright, even though he probably wouldn't have believed me. For him, words no longer held any value. His truth became only that which was tangible. His innocence was taken by the harsh realities of life. What tragic event has to happen in someone's life for their persona to be monumentally altered? Can they ever get it back?

My mind was still racing as I addressed the audience about how life had come full circle. I began my presentation by talking about how FEW and I were connected.

I had just finished the first phase of the tour and was packing up the remainder of my things at Nick's house. As I was packing, I found my mentor's award that was given to her by FEW. It had been a long day and I decided to take a break. I sat on the couch in the living room and noticed the award on the coffee table. I stared at it and thought, *Roy, you should email FEW.*

I ran to get my laptop, plugged it in, and grabbed a notepad and pen as I waited for it to load up. I googled Federally Employed Women's Conference. Instantly their website came up. I clicked on their site and began reading more about the organization. The only thing I knew at that point was I had stolen a meal from them. I began searching for as many emails as I could find and composed the following message.

Sent: Sat Jul 03 00:56:11 2010
Subject: FEW Inspiring Thousands of Teens Across the Country due to HBC - Tour

Greetings President and FEW Leaders,

In 1997 the FEW conference was in its 28th year and took place in Dallas, TX on July 7th-11th. That year your organization hired LTC (Retired) Consuelo Castillo Kickbusch to be a keynote speaker. While everyone was so busy making sure that things were in order, the participants were filling in the conference room preparing for dinner; no one noticed the homeless 16-year-old boy (me) who snuck in for a free meal.

What I received that day was much more than a meal! I know I didn't belong there, and I am sorry for eating a meal that wasn't mine but please forgive me... please keep reading.

I am now a college graduate from Hardin-Simmons University and business owner of a human development company. I have decided to pay it forward, and for two years I am circling the country on a national tour called; MyBag, MyHome: Homeless by Choice Tour with a goal of inspiring over 100,000 students with a message not to give up on life, their dreams, and understand the value of higher education!

Please visit the tour website. If there is a way, we can partner together and inspire the great group of women you work with and their children. I am more than willing. It is my goal to inspire as many people as possible.

Thank you very much for your time!

Sincerely,

Roy Juarez Jr.
Homeless by Choice Tour
www.HomelessbyChoice.com

I glanced at my mentor from the stage, hoping to receive some nonverbal feedback for my presentation. She sat there with a huge smile, like a proud mother. It was just the boost of confidence that I needed.

I continued, "When I sent your organization the email, I wasn't sure of what to expect. Honestly, I didn't think anything would come of it, I just thought it would be nice to share. So, you can imagine my surprise when I received an email back from Sue, forgiving me for stealing a meal. That night, fourteen years ago, you saved me," I looked over at Sue and gave her a smile.

"As a kid, I never wanted to be a speaker. I wanted to be a geologist, an astronaut, or a lawyer, but all those dreams were taken from me. Well, let me rephrase that; my environment convinced me to give all my dreams away and I didn't even realize it. When I walked into your conference, in 1997, I sat in the very far back corner."

I pointed to the section and said, "You, ma'am, in the corner with the white blouse. Where you are sitting, that's exactly where I sat. The night I snuck in, there weren't any guards at the door checking for meal tickets as there was today."

The audience started laughing.

"That night, you all showed me compassion and mercy, without even knowing it. Because of that, today I get to stand before you as a college graduate and human rights activist. Once I graduated college, I knew I had to pay it forward because there was another hurting 'Roy' out there somewhere, who was ready to give up. You taught me it only takes a FEW to care. It only takes a FEW to make a difference, and I want to be a part of that FEW."

I paused for a moment, and several people in the audience started to applaud.

"Please, allow me to share the accounts of my life with you this evening. I know we aren't connected by career, nor am I in the military, but we are connected by the human spirit…"

For the rest of the talk, I continued to open up my heart and pour every emotion out that it took to get me to that stage. I shared how I was abandoned, molested, invisible, and dismissed, and how my life took a turn when someone was willing to walk the journey with me, to get me back on a healthy path. Someone who was willing to see past all my flaws, and view life through my eyes. To help them understand, I told them the story of the Oreo cookies.

***

I had been working for my mentor for several months when she asked me to go with her to the grocery store. I gladly joined because I loved spending time with her, no matter where it was.

When we arrived at H.E.B., San Antonio's best grocery store, she said, "Mijo go get us a basket." When I returned with the basket, she gave me a list of items we needed for the house. She then added, "Make sure to get whatever you want too."

I thought, Whatever I want?

I rubbed my hands together as I imagined all the things I could fill the basket with. I could have taken anything in the entire store, but there was only one delicious snack I had in mind.

As we made our way up and down the aisles, I knew what I wanted, and was just waiting till we got there. Finally, we walked down the cookie aisle, and my eyes scanned the shelf, looking for the bright blue and white wrapping. There they were, my favorite cookies, Oreos. I know she said I could have whatever I wanted, but I was still scared to put them in the basket.

Just to make sure, I asked, "Mrs. K, can I get Oreos?"

"Of course mijo, get the double stuffed."

Her words put a huge smile on my face. You would have thought I was an eight-year-old kid. Deep down, it was the broken eight-year-old who wanted the cookies that he never had. Regardless, I grabbed the double stuffed packet and placed them in the cart. We continued to shop until we had everything on our list.

As we made our way home, all I could think about were my cookies. We got to Mrs. K's house and unloaded everything; however, I made sure to put my cookies aside. I took them to the office and grabbed a sticky note. On the note, I wrote, "Roy's Cookies - Don't Touch!!!" I looked at the warning proudly, stuck it to the Oreos, then placed them in the food pantry before I headed back to the office and continued working.

It wasn't very long before Mrs. K walked in and said, "Roy, can I speak with you in the kitchen?"

I thought, Crap, I'm in trouble.

I didn't know what I had done wrong. Every time Mrs. K wanted to have a "mentoring" session with me, it was at the kitchen table.

I grabbed a notepad and pen, just in case, and hesitantly walked down the short hallway where I could see her sitting at the table, with my cookies right in front of her. I sat down, still confused. I wanted to know what I did wrong, but I was scared to ask. She slid the Oreos over, so that they were directly between us.

Finally, I mustered up the courage to ask, "Ma'am, am I in trouble? Did I do something wrong?"

Mrs. K smiled and said, "No Roy, you are not in trouble."

A weight lifted off my shoulders. At that time, I was scared of Ms. K; I never wanted to see her go colonel. I had witnessed it a few times and understood why the Army loved her so much.

She said, "Mijo, I noticed you put a note on these cookies."

I dropped my head in shame because I knew I *did* do something wrong.

In a loving voice, she said, "Mijo, look at me, you're not in trouble. When these cookies are gone, I promise you, I will get you more."

I sat in silence, but I knew what she was trying to say.

"Will it be okay for me to take off the note, so all the family could share them?" she continued.

"Yes ma'am, I'm sorry. We can remove the note," I said, forcing a smile through my embarrassment.

"Great!"

She removed the note and asked me to put the cookies back in the pantry.

It wasn't until years later that she explained herself, saying, "Mijo, remember that time I bought you Oreo cookies?"

I laughed, "Yes ma'am, I remember."

"Did I ever tell you my thought process about that incident?"

"No, ma'am, but I get it now. I was selfish."

My mentor disagreed, "No, no you weren't. You were a broken, homeless young man. Roy, when I first saw that note on those cookies, I got upset. I thought you were ungrateful. I thought, *you didn't even pay for these cookies how could you demand the family not eat them?* Then I had to stop myself, do you know why?"

A lump began to form in my throat because I still felt terrible about it. I forced a reply to her rhetorical question, "No ma'am, I don't know why."

"I stopped myself because I was looking at the situation through my lens, a middle-class lens. I wasn't looking at the situation through your lens. Those were your favorite cookies, and I'm sure with your upbringing you didn't always get your favorite anything. I had to look through your lens, so I could understand why you wrote the note."

Even though her words were teaching me a lesson about life, I couldn't help but feel sad about it.

I tried to apologize again, "Ma'am, I am so sorry I cam—"

She interrupted, "Mijo, don't be sorry. I am sorry I first failed to understand you. Mijo, as you become a leader and eventually have your own mentees, employees, and even with your family, learn to see life through their lens; don't be so quick to judge."

***

Again, I looked back at Mrs. K sitting in the audience and noticed she was wiping tears from her eyes. As I finished my story, I reiterated, "It was that wisdom, and the wisdom from every person who was willing to help me navigate my life, that I get to stand before you today."

Thinking back to my youth, there were a few individuals who truly made a difference in my life that I haven't mentioned but are equally important. Individuals like my aunt Rosa Martinez and her family who hid us from my father. The Teague family who didn't really know us but showed us so much kindness. Rhonda Hughes and her sons Ryan and Al, who clothed me and treated me like family for as long as they could. It was the Regan Blaufarbs of the world, who would sneak me into their house, feed me, and give me a place to sleep. It only takes a few to make all the difference.

I closed my presentation by sharing these final thoughts with the audience, "It wouldn't be right not to acknowledge the special woman in this room. Fourteen years ago, I snuck into your conference as a homeless teenager and stole a meal. For that, I am sorry. Today, I am an activist and college graduate because it only took a FEW to care. I would like to welcome the woman who cared enough, even when others told her to get rid of me. Please welcome my mentor, Retired Lieutenant Colonel Consuelo Castillo Kickbusch."

The audience gave her a huge round of applause as she made her way to the stage. As soon as she got to me, she hugged me tightly and whispered in my ear, "I am so proud of you mijo." I handed her the microphone, but she didn't say a word, she stood there, with her back straight and puffed in pride, cradling the mic to her chest. She pivoted to face the audience as she extended her hand, as if to present me.

She said, "I present, Mr. Roy Juarez Jr., the son I've always wished for."

This was one of the best nights on tour. It wouldn't have been possible without the help of; Sue Webster, the National President; Suzi Inman, the National Training Program (NTP) 2011 Chair; and Joyce Hageman, who lead FEW's first ever youth event outreach team.

## Central Catholic High School

James and I drove into Pittsburgh, Pennsylvania, not knowing what to expect. We were headed to meet Susy Robinson from the Homeless Children Education Fund, a Non-Profit established in 1999 to support the educational needs of children experiencing homelessness in Allegheny County.

James and I were able to partner with their organization as they helped us secure schools for me to speak at. Through that partnership, I was able to meet Mrs. Liza Zimmerman, the then Program manager for Healthy Start, a transitional living home for women and children experiencing homelessness. We hit it off so well that Liza and her husband were kind enough to take James and me in for the night. I have a fond memory of her 6-year-old daughter, Jade, playing with my hair and filling it with multi-colored hair barrettes. Her husband, Rich, and James couldn't stop laughing.

The next day, I was set to speak at Central Catholic High School, a college preparatory for boys. My nerves were in overdrive for this presentation because it was my first time speaking to an audience comprised of all teenage boys.

We arrived early at the campus because the brothers of the church allowed us to stay with them for a night. The building's architecture reminded me of something out of the Harry Potter movies. The entrance to the school was nestled between two drum towers that stood five stories tall. The entire structure was built in coppertone and black-diamond colored bricks. Throughout the interior of the school, the black-diamond bricks were used to create small cross-shaped designs on the walls.

We made our way to the front office where we met with Principal Robert Schaefer, better known as Brother Bob. He was a delightful man with rosy red cheeks, round face, and bald on top. He greeted us with a warm smile and firm handshake. After a brief conversation about the school and history of Central Catholic, he walked us over to the rectory. I had no clue what a rectory was until that day. A rectory is where the priests live and where James and I would now be staying. It was just as beautiful as the rest of the campus. As Brother Bob checked us in, he handed us separate keys because we each had our own rooms.

I looked over at James, and teased, "Finally, I'll have some privacy!"

"Yeah right, I'm the one who's been trying to get away from *you*!"

We both walked to our rooms and after settling in, James and I made our way back to the school campus. The students were already filling the McGonigle Theatre as James and I walked in. I was blown away by how beautiful the theatre looked! The walls were comprised of aged red brick and stained glasses windows. The stage was framed with a high pointed arch. The ceiling was checkered with burnt orange and royal blue squares, and in each of the orange squares was a knight's shield with a cross on them.

Walking towards the front, where our seats had been saved, I was able to see that the theatre was filled to the brim. After a few minutes of waiting, Brother Bob walked on stage and silence fell over the audience; the boys didn't dare speak while he was up there. In a deep, stern voice, that was frightening to even me; he said, "I expect you all to be on your best behavior, remember God is in this place, and He is watching you."

I slowly turned to James with wide eyes and whispered, "I've never spoken for God before."

I wasn't even trying to be funny. Brother Bob put the fear of God in me.

As he came off the stage, I approached him and asked, "Brother Bob, can I share with you a little about my presentation?"

"You will be fine," he replied.

"Yes, Brother, but there are a few jokes I tell during my presentation I would like to run by you."

"I am sure they will be fine," he said again as he nudged me towards the stage.

Brother Bob had just introduced me before walking off and didn't want the stage to be empty for long, but I was too scared to go on without his blessing.

"Are you *sure* brother?" I asked one more time.

He didn't answer but nodded his head.

I walked up the stairs and gave myself a mental pep talk, *You got this, Roy.* The presentation was a huge success.

Afterward, as a crowd of students headed to the stage, the Brothers of Central Catholic approached me and asked, "How can we help you on your mission?"

James and I looked at each other, and said simultaneously, "We really need a place to stay."

"Not a problem. You gentleman are welcome to stay with us as long as you need and anytime you find yourself in the area. Is there anything else?"

I spoke, alone this time, "Brother, it would really help the tour if we could sell wristbands during lunch. Would that be okay with you?"

"Certainly! We will schedule it for tomorrow, so we can inform the boys to bring money if they're interested."

"Thank you, Brother Bob!"

I turned my attention to what was now a line of students waiting to talk to me. I met so many great young men. However, during our conversations, the same question kept coming up: "Have you met Brother Kenneth?" I wasn't sure who Brother Kenneth was, but it was obvious he had made an impression with the students.

That evening, James and I were sitting in the rectory library when a brother whom we hadn't met walked in, he was wearing the same garment as all the other brothers, a long black robe and a white clerical collar. He approached us and said, "Hi, I'm Brother Kenneth."

"Oh wow! It nice to finally meet you, Brother Kenneth. I heard plenty about you today."

"Well, don't believe it. Unless it was good stuff, then of course it's true."

James and I laughed.

"Brother, it was all good," James reassured.

"So," Brother Kenneth started as he turned towards me, "were you the young man that spoke today? I have heard a lot about you."

"Yes sir, that was me."

"Tell me, what do you do on this tour when you aren't speaking?"

"Well, my assistant and I do all kinds of things to keep ourselves busy when we have some free time."

"Like what?" he inquired.

"We've been able to visit capital buildings, museums, caves, —"

"Caves? Why caves?"

"Because they're fun, it's dark, cold, and there are bats!"

"Dark and cold? Sounds like my heart!"

James and I busted out laughing.

We now knew why the students loved Brother Kenneth so much, he was a funny man. Since it was getting late, after a few minutes conversing, Brother Kenneth excused himself. James and I did the same and made our way to our rooms. As I was preparing for the next day, I realized I only had a couple wristbands left to sell. It wouldn't be enough to raise money for the tour since I only sold them for $3 each, so I had to think of an idea quick. I texted James and asked if he wanted to go to Walmart with me. Surely there would be something I could find there to help me raise some money for the tour.

At Walmart, I purchased a canvas board and paint markers and prayed my idea wouldn't fail me. In my room that night, I painted "Be the Change" in bold blue letters on the canvas. The next morning, as a fundraiser, the students could buy a wristband if there were any available or, for $5, they could sign the canvas as a way to show they helped create change. By the end of lunch, the tour had raised over $1,000.

I will be forever grateful to boys of Central Catholic for helping keep the tour alive.

The Pittsburgh area is an extraordinary place. We found the same love and acceptance from the students of Serra Catholic and the Kramer family.

## Falls Church, Virginia – 22 Months into the Tour

I had just finished speaking at J.E.B. Stuart High School, home of the Raiders. Their entire student body was squeezed into the gym. The students, who didn't fit on the bleachers, sat in chairs that were set up on the basketball court or stood along the back wall. I presented on a small platform in the middle of the gym. I felt like I was Shakespeare performing theater-in-the-round.

After leaving the school, it wasn't long before the rush faded. The pressures of the tour were pushing down on my shoulders. I needed to get some thoughts out of my mind. So, I decided that I would drive and let James play on Facebook. There were only a few months left of the tour, and the journey had been extremely challenging. It definitely would have been worse if it wasn't for James joining me again!

I thought out loud, "Even with all my childhood traumatic experiences, I still had some great times with my family."

James looked up from his phone and asked, "Are you talking to me?"

"Fool, you're the only one here," I laughed, hiding the fact that I just talked to myself like I was crazy.

"Well I don't know, you get all weird every time we leave a school."

James had a point; my emotions always ran high after I presented.

He put his phone down and said, "Fine, tell me your story, but I'm not gonna give you a donation."

"What I was saying was, my siblings and I had some good times too, even though life sucked. I mean, we were close, but I still feel a separation between us. If anyone thinks I have it all together, they couldn't be further from the truth."

"I never thought you had it all together, I know how screwed you are," James laughed.

"Let me finish, stupid," I said jokingly. "All I'm trying to do is be the best person I can be, to be kind and hopefully inspire others. I guess the question I've been trying to answer this entire tour is, *who am I?*"

"Mijo, you're a good person. You're THE Roy Juarez Jr.," James continued to taunt me.

"James! I'm gonna pull over and leave you here!"

"I wish you would," he chuckled. "Okay, okay, I'll listen. Talk."

For the next few minutes I talked to James about how I was feeling. I knew this journey started out so that I could help kids, but it really made me question my own existence, my purpose, my legacy. I know I wanted to figure out who I was. This hasn't come to me easily, but does it come easily for anyone? I am still on this journey to figure that out and I firmly believe that it will be a lifelong pilgrimage. Hopefully, I won't die trying to figure it out on this tour, there are some crazy drivers out here. Some jerk had cut me off, I wanted to yell, "Use your darn blinker!"

"Do you want me to drive? I'm not ready to die," James asked.

"No, he cut me off! I'm a better driver than you anyway."

"Oh, okay, that's crap. I can drive better than you with my eyes closed."

"Shut up, let me finish. What kind of best friend are you?"

"Fine, keep crying, I mean talking."

As we drove further I continued to bore James, talking about everything I could remember. I told him the story that went like this…

From a very young age, I had a strong desire to understand who I was and what I believed in. I wanted to feel like I belonged. Sometimes, I envied those who cared less about the state of others or who were satisfied with the status quo. It's not that they are settling, because success means something different to us all.

For some, success is having a stable job and a family; others may want a high paying job, and a few just want to serve. Neither idea of success is above the other, just different.

There is nothing wrong with wanting a high paying job or wanting to be able to afford the finer things in life, as long as you aren't chasing those things to feed the fractured child buried deep inside of you. We must be able to be happy even if we have nothing, as that's what true happiness is. For me, life is all about figuring out who you want to be and working towards becoming that person.

Many people go through their entire life without ever really living a single day. Some are born into a broken environment, accepted the lessons taught to them, and never reached their full potential because they were puppets to someone else's brokenness.

I often wonder if my dad is a victim of this cycle. There had to be a time when he was 7 years old and had dreams about who he wanted to be and where he wanted to go in life. But somewhere along the way, life happened—by way of other people's brokenness—and it broke him. He didn't even realize it, and unintentionally, he began teaching the same lessons to his children.

I've noticed something on this tour though, and I find it very interesting. I actually believe it could be an epidemic in our society. Everyone always blames my mom for what happened to us. They are always angry at her and question, "How could a mother leave her kids?" But no one ever asks about my father or puts any blame on him. It's like no one even expected him to be in the picture in the first place. That is a scary thought, *are the youth in America so used to absent fathers that we don't even consider them as part of the problem?* Have we come to accept that it's "normal" for them to walk away from their responsibility as a father. In which kids are left with this empty void, hoping their dad would love them one day, causing them years of unsurfaced trauma.

I once said to my sister, "I have seen how ugly you can be towards mom, but when it comes to dad, you're very careful with your words because you don't want to hurt him and cause him any pain. I'm not saying we should hurt dad, but why is it okay to hurt mom? The one who has been there for you the most and the longest. Mom doesn't deserve that!"

My father wouldn't even accept responsibility. Once, I tried to have a conversation with him, and he said, "It's not my fault you were homeless, it's your mother's fault. You were living with her at the time." Even though we were in hiding from him.

What happened to my siblings and me wasn't just my mother's fault, but in my culture, for whatever reason, we put more blame on our mothers than we do our fathers and that is not right! My father had a whole lot to do with this. My mother stayed as long as she could and came back. It's definitely something we should all put thought to.

Regardless, I find myself in my thirties, undoing the damage of my youth. A person shouldn't have to spend their adult life undoing the damage of their childhood just to start their life.

Then there are other individuals I've meet on the road; the students, the host families who take me in, my interns, and they've all become my family too. I love them very much, but I think I need them more than they need me. They give me a sense of acceptance and love. It makes all the pain I went through growing up have purpose. For the longest time, I was just faithing it, hoping to make it. It was in those darkest hours of my life, when I felt utterly alone, that I had to rely purely on my belief in God.

When I became a youth pastor for the second time, I was 18 years old. I would often tell my staff the same thing, "You have to faith it, till you make it." I didn't mean the cliché "Fake it till you make it." I believe those two sayings have entirely different meanings.

Faking something means that you might not believe in what you are doing, but you still do it for the results. However, when you faith it, you believe in what you are doing wholeheartedly. You don't even have to see the end result because you believe it's already there. There will be days that we will not feel like ourselves, and that's okay. We just have to give our best, whatever our best is for that day.

James jumped in and said, "It reminds me of that analogy you told me about, with Michael Jordan."

"Yes! Exactly."

I once heard a story about Michael Jordan. I am not sure about the validity of the story, but I liked the message. I don't remember who told me, but it went like this, "Michael Jordan once said, 'the world has this expectation of who Michael Jordan is... when I don't feel like Michael Jordan, I don't leave my house. When I feel like Michael Jordan, I venture out...'"

While Michael Jordan may have the means to choose to stay home when he doesn't feel like himself, that's not the reality for the majority of us.

Others like me, and probably you, must leave every day to make a living, but how can we take the same message and apply it to our lives? We can faith it till we make it by identifying our core values and putting them into action on days where we don't feel like our best self.

Growing up as a homeless teenager can really strip you of an identity. You get lost in the streets of survival by becoming whoever and whatever others want you to be. Even if you try to hold on to your identity, the need is real. It becomes easy to throw your values out the window when you're hungry. It is during these times of trial and tribulation that we have to try our hardest to remember our values. It is in those tough moments that our character is tested and shaped. This is why we have to decide who we want to be and work towards that consciously.

I finished my storytelling flurry with, "James, the crazy thing is, all the work I'm doing keeps my old memories and emotions alive. I'm always reminding myself to separate the anger and bitterness from those memories. It's one thing to remember the past and another to live in it."

Eventually, once I finished venting, I looked to James for a response. He was asleep! That jerk.

# CHAPTER SIXTEEN

## I'm Still Standing

### Bethlehem, New Hampshire - 27 Months into the Tour

AS JAMES AND I were driving south on I-93, I was worried about losing signal. My phone kept fluctuating between no service and two bars. When I eventually had three bars, I instructed him to pull over and park, so we could wait for the call I was expecting. I was nervous and excited. It was a phone interview that would be broadcasted live on five different radio stations across the state of Michigan. It would bring great coverage to the tour.

Finally, the phone rang, and I quickly answered it. Someone from the radio station gave me a brief run-through of how the process would go and then transferred me over to Ray Leonard.

"Hey Roy, it's Ray Leonard here. First off, I want to thank you for taking the time to come on to the show," he said in an enthusiastic voice.

"Of course sir, I'm glad I'm able to be on your show and share information about the Homeless by Choice tour with you."

As the interview began, Mr. Leonard immediately started asking me questions about my childhood. He wasted no time with surface level conversation but dug deep with thought-provoking questions about my past. After a couple of questions, I noticed my hands getting sweaty and my leg shaking uncontrollably. I wasn't prepared for what he was asking and felt myself becoming more anxious after each question he asked. The time between my answers and his next question were dreadful.

"Roy, let me get this straight. By the age of 14, you had already been rejected by countless adults. Your dad didn't want you, your mom didn't want you, your grandparents didn't want you, not even your aunts and uncles wanted you. Nobody wanted you."

I paused for what felt like hours. I had never thought about it like that before. His words cut me deep. I remember him trying to make a joke to make light of the story, but there was so much truth in what he just said. The people in my life who were supposed to love me, care for me, or just be there for me had rejected me. Now, as an adult, I was able to analyze the reasoning behind his question, but at 14 years old there was so much I didn't understand.

When I was 14, I wasn't able to make this connection, and I believe it was a godsend. Growing up, I had managed to push questions like these into my subconscious. But during that interview, at 30 years old, I was able to make the connection, and it hit me like a ton of bricks. I sat there, still silent, with my phone pressed hard against my ear.

"Roy? You still there?" I heard Mr. Leonard's voice from the other end.

"Yes sir, I'm still here," I said as I pulled myself together to keep the interview going.

After the interview, James and I swapped seats. The questions Ray Leonard asked me replayed over and over in my mind as I drove through the darkness of the night. Affected by reliving what happened to me in my adolescent years, I persisted in trying to figure out how my past made me feel. *In what deep corners of my mind was I able to hide away the awful memories? How did I let go?* That is, if I even had let go.

All the questions I had suppressed before the interview suddenly emerged as I drove to the next city. As James slept, it was just me and the dark open road for hours upon hours. As much as I would have preferred to sleep, to keep myself from overthinking, I had to fight to stay awake because I needed to make my next presentation in the morning. That's when it hit me.

I was traveling all across the country with a dream of making life better for others, while I was struggling to hold myself together. I tried to be something for everyone else, to help them on my Homeless by Choice journey but realized it was turning into more of a pilgrimage. The tour was allowing me to take the time to understand who I was and, in doing that, an awareness of a deep-rooted internal conflict arose.

I was torn between my passion and commitment to my family; my mom, my siblings, and my nieces. Was I letting them all down? I must have been because every time I received a text message from one of my siblings, sharing yet another milestone in the family that I missed again, I felt like a failure to them all.

My younger sister, Danielle, would send a text message saying, "Jaden took her first step!" Then my older sister Tammy would send me a text, proud that Keirsten, my niece, just hit another home run. Another message from my older sister Amy, trying to keep me in the loop, would be a picture of her daughter Mia, who was growing so fast. All of them were growing up without knowing their uncle.

This drive seemed to drag on much longer than others. In my last endeavor to try to shake these thoughts from my mind, I remembered a text one of my siblings had sent me a couple of months prior. It was as if I was reading it for the first time again. "You've already helped enough people out there. We miss you too, and whether you care or not, we want you home." A lump began to form in my throat, and the road blurred with every blink.

What are we really chasing in life? Oftentimes we get caught up in "chasing" a better life, a better partner, a better job. When we spend so much time chasing, we forget to live in the moment, and life can easily pass us by. It took me living homeless for the second time to see clearly that I was loved. Maybe not by everyone, but by the right ones. I wasn't going to find happiness in others or materialistic things, but I needed to find happiness in myself. This journey pushed me to my limits, but I was still standing.

## Bridgeport, Connecticut - 29 Months into the Tour

The phone rang several times before my mother answered. As always, she said, "Hi mijo, how are you doing?" I could hardly contain myself.

Excited, I replied, "Hey mom, I'm doing well! What are you doing?"

"I'm at work. Where are you at?" she asked.

Traveling from state to state so often, my mom never really knew where I was.

"Right now James and I are in Bridgeport, Connecticut. We got here a couple of days ago."

Surprised, she continued with her questions, "Connecticut? What are y'all doing way up there?"

I chuckled and said, "I just finished speaking at an afterschool program called Lighthouse, but that's not the reason I'm calling. I wanted to ask, what are you doing this coming Tuesday, May 8th? I was going to see if you could take the day off."

"I'm working mijo, why? Is everything okay? What's going on?" I could tell the suspense was making her anxious, so I told her the news without pause.

"Mom, as of today, the tour has reached 99,632 people! Can you believe that? My next event is Tuesday, May 8th at the University of Toledo. They're having their 10th Annual Latino Youth Summit and expecting about 650 people. That means I'm gonna reach my goal of speaking to over 100,000 people! Can you believe it?"

The excitement in my mom's voice matched my own, "Oh my God! Really? Wow mijo, that's great! I'll ask my boss right now. Hold on, don't hang up!"

"Wait, mom! You need to ask for the 7th and 8th off because I have to fly you here and back," I said as quickly as possible before she put down the phone.

As I sat there waiting, James asked, "Is she coming?"

"I don't know, she's asking her boss now," I said, crossing my fingers that my mother would be able to join us for such a significant milestone in the tour. I could hear her in the distance talking to her boss but couldn't clearly make out what they were saying to each other.

I really hoped her boss would let her come. I thought about the potential power of the message it could have on the students if she were with me. Beyond that, the bonding moment my mother and I would share would mean so much after all we had been through.

Then I heard movement from the other line and her voice came through the phone once again.

"Mijo, he said I can have time off. What do I need to do? How do I book my flight?" she asked.

"Mom, you don't have to do anything. I'll book your flight and send you all the information that you need. I'll talk to you later, okay? I have to make my way to Ohio in a bit," I replied.

"Oh! I am so excited, thank you mijo! Also, be careful! Let me know when you're in Ohio, so I know you're safe. Love you."

"I love you too, mom. I'll see you soon," I said just as we hung up the phone.

I couldn't believe that—after all this time, effort, and energy—the big day was a week away. Even though I was going to hit my goal of speaking to over 100,000 individuals; that wasn't going to be the last event on the Homeless by Choice Tour.

I wanted to reach several thousand more just in case my estimation was off. After the 10th Annual Latino Youth Summit, I had twelve more events lined up, and my estimated final headcount was a little over 108,000 individuals. A dream come true.

James and I had time to waste, so instead of driving straight to Toledo, we stopped to visit our friend Jesse Ontiveros in Washington, D.C. The only downfall of staying with him was he made me work out all the time. I needed it, but I was so tired. James liked to pretend he could keep up, but I call bull-crap. We were both out of shape.

After our mini vacation, we finally made it to Toledo, Ohio and met up with my good friend, Adrian Calderon, from the United States Hispanic Leadership Institute (USHLI). USHLI was the organization sponsoring my presentation and was generous enough to have Adrian book us a hotel. James and I checked in and unloaded our things before heading to pick up my mother from the airport. It had been a couple of months since I last saw her, so I decided to surprise her with flowers and dinner at Buffalo Wild Wings. Don't judge me, it's a great place when on the Homeless by Choice Tour!

Once I picked her up, she gave James and I a huge hug. We could tell how excited she was to be with us. She couldn't stop talking about her flight and how scary it was. I laughed.

As soon as we got into the car, I asked, "Are you hungry?"

She replied, "I can eat."

"Perfect," I said and drove straight to the restaurant.

James and I sat there talking to my mom about all the people we had met on our travels. James asked, "Did you tell her about the earthquake in D.C. when we were staying with Jesse? Or how we lost power in New York because of the Nor'easter and had to use a windup flashlight for light when we pooped?"

"Gross James!" My mom laughed. "And a windup flashlight?"

"What Mama Rosa? You don't poop?" James lovingly teased with his mouth full.

"Don't pay attention to him, mom. Yeah, the entire hotel was pitch black! Actually, every hotel for miles had lost electricity."

"It was freezing too!" James added.

"Well, I'm sure you didn't mind the cold mijo."

"No mom! I was freezing!"

"Oh my God, my poor babies! Well, I am glad the tour is almost over."

"Me too!" said James, "I need a real job that pays!"

We had finished dinner and the waitress brought us our check. I was a little upset that my mom wouldn't let me pay because I wanted to treat her.

"Mijo, save your money," she insisted.

After dinner, we made our way back to the hotel where we stayed the rest of the evening. My mother and I sat in the room playing Candy Crush together all night. She's addicted, but I enjoyed hearing her laugh and giggle each time we beat a level.

The next morning, we made our way to the university for the event. I was elated because this was going to be my finish line. Even though it was the Latino Youth Summit, in my mind, all the attendees would be there to help me celebrate the huge milestone of the tour.

While I spoke, I made sure to soak up every detail as I looked out into the audience. The enormous room was filled with round tables, draped in black cloths. Positioned near the stage sat my mother, trying not to bring attention to herself. I could tell she was trying to hold herself together while listening to me rehash my adolescence. My beautiful mother, with her fair skin and dark hair that came down to her shoulders, was wiping tears from her eyes. Each time we made eye contact, she gave me a broken smile filled with pain and regret. But I could tell she wanted me to know that it was okay to keep sharing.

When I was close to the end of my presentation, I said to the audience, "I don't know who you are or what you've been through, but I do know we all have a story. If your journey requires you to forgive, take that first step with me today by forgiving my mother."

I turned towards my mother and asked her to join me on stage. The audience held their breath. Students in the back jumped up from their seats, trying to get a glimpse of her. She stood up and slowly made her way to stage as I continued.

"I'd like to introduce to you my beautiful mother," I announced as the crowd began to applaud. She joined me, tears still streaming down her face. I wrapped my arms around her, and whispered in her ear, "It's okay, you're okay."

With my arm wrapped around my mother's shoulder, I continued, "Let me tell you something about parents. They are human. They hurt like we hurt, they make mistakes like we make mistakes. We can be the ones to love them past their brokenness." I questioned the students in the audience, "When was the last time you went home to your mother or father, whoever that may be, and asked them 'How can I make your day better?' I've come to learn that family isn't just the blood that flows through our veins, but it's the love in our hearts. Whether it's your grandmother, grandfather, uncle, aunt, or whoever you consider your parent, when was the last time you went home and asked, 'How are you feeling today?' Parents are human, they break. We have to be the change that we want to see in our family, but that change starts with us."

I gave my mother one last kiss on the crown of her head and said to the audience, "Thank you for having us, I hope you take something from this humble message."

Together, we walked off stage.

## Back at the Waffle House

"The event finished around 2:00 pm, so I was able to spend some time with my mom before I had to drop her off at the airport. I started my drive home and ended up here 'cause I was hungry," I smiled.

"Wait, where's James?" Morgan asked with concern in her voice.

I laughed, "He weak. He's sleeping in the car. I tried to wake him up when we got here, but he wanted to sleep."

"Awe, I wish I could have met him," she said before changing the subject. "Roy, I don't know what to say. Thank you for sharing your journey with me. You're right; every person has a story of their own. You just never know."

"Yeah, there are a lot of people hurting out there. There's so much anger and hatred around, we shouldn't add to it."

Just then, I asked the waitress for my bill. It was getting late, I was tired, and James was still passed out in the car. Before I left, Morgan and I exchanged contact information.

I walked out of the diner and got back into my car, accidentally waking up James.

He looked over at me and asked, still half asleep, "Did you get me anything? I'm hungry."

"Seriously?"

"Naw, I'm joking. Just get me to a hotel," James said as he put his head back down.

I found the closest hotel and used the money my mother had given us to rest for the night.

The next morning, I woke up to a text from Morgan.

It read: "Hey Roy, I was wondering if you were still in town. If you are, I'd love to meet at the Waffle House for breakfast, I have something for you."

I replied to her and told her I could be there in an hour. I was surprised she had something to give me. What could it be?

I woke up James and said, "Hey, get ready. We're going to meet Morgan for breakfast."

"Who the hell is Morgan?" he asked.

I just laughed and left it at that.

When we walked into the Waffle House, Morgan was sitting in a corner booth. She stood up and walked over to me. We gave each other a hug. The look on James' face was priceless, he had no idea what was going on.

Morgan extended her hand towards James and said, "Hi, I'm—"

"The famous Morgan," James said as he hesitated to shake her hand.

"Yes, Morgan. You must be James. Roy and I met last night while you were sleeping in the car," she laughed while trying to explain.

"Cool, let's eat," James replied, clearly too hungry for introductions.

We walked back to the booth where she was sitting.

"Roy, I asked you to meet me here because I was thinking about everything you said, and it's so true. Everyone has a story, everyone has a past. How weird it must be for someone to forget that. I mean, it's always with you, you never lose it. You might forget it, but it's always with you. I guess what I am trying to say is, the past and the future correlate with one another, like puzzle pieces. It's just funny how everything comes together."

She continued, "My freshman year, while on winter break, I painted a picture on a piece of cardboard. I was so moved by your words last night and your willingness to share a piece of yourself with me. I'd like to give you the painting and share a piece of myself with you. Maybe you can use it when you talk to the kids."

Morgan reached under the table and grabbed a large object wrapped in butcher paper. She placed it in front of me on the table.

"Open it!" she smiled.

Excited, I ripped off the butcher paper from the front of the painting. Staring at me was a beautiful portrait of Mohandas K. Gandhi. I was enamored.

"Morgan, this is absolutely stunning! I'm speechless!"

Morgan continued, "I was thinking about everything you told me last night, about the tour..." she spoke slowly, "But what I couldn't figure out was, how you became homeless? There's still so much you left out of your story."

I grinned at her and said, "How about we save that story for another time?"

# EPILOGUE:

## My Motivation

WHEN I BEGAN writing this section, I had no clue where to start. I love my siblings with all my heart, but I found it difficult to remember our past. I know we've had good times, but I couldn't remember any of them. I even texted my siblings and asked, "Hey, what was your favorite memory of us?"

Amy replied, "Remember when my windshield wipers didn't work, and you hung out the window to manually do it as I drove?"

Baby Ray noted, "When you took me on that college road trip!"

Tammy said, "I don't think you want my favorite memory in your book."

Oh God… she was right.

Then, Danielle said, "I can't remember a happy childhood memory with you."

Which broke my heart.

I knew we had some good times, so I laid down and tried to resurface as many good memories as I could. I didn't want recent memories, I wanted memories from our childhood. I decided to create an environment of relaxation and peace, so I dimmed the lights in my house. I downloaded some calm music and began to write, allowing myself to roam the subconscious corners of my mind.

As I closed my eyes, I was taken back to a time when I was 7 years old. I remember waking up in my room from the thunder that was roaring outside my window. I was terrified of thunderstorms because I always thought a tornado was coming to get me. Actually, it's embarrassing to admit, but thunderstorms are still one of my biggest fears.

As a little boy, I used to run to the room my sisters shared. When I was lucky, one of them would let me crawl into their bed. When I wasn't, I would seek shelter under their bed to feel safe. As I laid on the floor, I couldn't help but worry that the tornado would come and take my sisters. So, I would crawl out, like a soldier on patrol, and make my way to every window in the house. I was waiting for the lighting to strike so I could get a glimpse of the sky. If a tornado were near, I'd be able to warn my family and give them enough time to take shelter.

With this behavior, you would have thought I had seen a tornado before or had some horrific encounter, but nope, I was just deathly scared of them. Even as a teenager, I used to loop my belts together and tie myself to the toilet because I was scared a tornado was going to take me away.

My sisters and brother are my everything. I couldn't imagine life without them. They are the main reason I work so hard and don't give up. Even though we fight like all other siblings, they are still my everything.

When I was in sixth grade, I was being bullied by another student in the hallway. Word got to my sister Tammy, who wasn't too far away, and she came running to where I was and jumped the other kid. As he ran away, my sister turned around to scold me, "And you! *You* need to learn to stick up for yourself!"

My response was, "God will fight my battles."

This really pissed her off, and she screamed, "God isn't %$#&ing here!"

I looked at her and said, "He sent you, didn't He?"

This is something we still laugh about.

My older sisters and I have more childhood memories because we still had each other. I didn't get to make the same memories with my youngest siblings, Danielle and Baby Ray, because of our homeless situation. When I was younger, all I wanted was to be around my older sisters, but they viewed me as the annoying little brother. My sister Tammy's best friend, Jennifer Duran, would say it the best, "He's such a nuisance." I think she had just learned that big word and I had no clue what it meant. I had to look it up in the dictionary. Luckily, she no longer sees me the same way, she sees how awesome I am. Just kidding.

I didn't mean to be a nuisance, I just wanted to be around them because I thought they were so cool. However, Tammy and Amy loved to gang up on me. We would often play a game made-up by my sisters called "Restaurant." The concept was simple, I would pretend to be a restaurant owner, and my sisters were the customers. They would walk into the dining room area, and I would be waiting for them with a napkin draped across my arm as I welcomed them to Roy's Bistro. I would show them to their table and pull the chair out for each of them as they sat.

I would run into the kitchen and serve them each a glass of water. After a few minutes, I would return with a notepad and pen to take their order. My sisters could order anything we had in the house. Usually, as an appetizer, I would serve them Saltine crackers with melted cheese on top. For dinner, they either ordered macaroni and cheese, Ramen Noodles, or a grilled cheese with fries.

I would run back into the kitchen and begin preparing whatever meal they ordered, periodically checking on them and refilling their drinks. Once their food was ready, I'd serve them both and clean the kitchen as they ate.

After they were done eating, it was time for the roles to reverse. Now, they would be the restaurant owners, and I would be the customer. I was excited because I knew exactly what I wanted to order. I made sure not to snack on the food I made them, so I wouldn't ruin my appetite.

Once the kitchen was clean, I made my way back to the table to find it empty. My sisters were in the room they shared, listening to music. Excited, I entered their room and said, "Okay, the kitchen is clean. I'm ready to be the customer!"

As they looked at each other and laughed, they both said, "We don't want to play that game anymore."

It made me so upset.

You would think I would have learned my lesson the first time, but nope! Each time they wanted to play Restaurant, I gladly joined in hoping it would be different, but it wasn't. I got duped every time.

Even though this story shows how evil they were (I am joking, we were kids), I honestly think I continued to play because I loved spending time with them. It didn't matter if I was serving them, I was with them.

My sister Amy is the oldest, and I often say, has the biggest heart out of all of us. She is definitely the most visibly sensitive one. I know my other sisters are sensitive too, but they don't like to show it.

A lot of my memories with Amy stem from our times at church. We were both youth leaders and in the choir. We had so many fun times at youth night, working with teens. From the plays we directed, to the lock-ins we organized, there was never a dull moment. Because my adopted parents were the pastors of the church, Amy grew very close to them as well.

On one occasion, she asked if she could come to spend the night at my adoptive parents' house. They agreed, and I was excited to spend more time with my sister. We all decided to stay up late and watch the movie *The Shining* based on the Stephen King novel. I think they chose that movie because they knew how terrified I was of scary movies.

During the movie, I reluctantly walked through the dining room, over to the kitchen, to get something to drink. As much as I wanted to turn on the lights, I didn't because we lived in the country on seven acres of land, and I worried someone in the woods would see me through the window if the lights were on. I quickly filled my glass and rushed back to the living room in the dark. Just as I passed the dining table, I heard a noise from behind me.

I picked up my pace before clearly hearing a demonic, "REDЯUM, REDЯUM," coming from the darkness.

I dropped my glass and ran back to the living room, screaming for my adoptive parents. They both sat on the couch, laughing at the terrified expression on my face. I scanned the living room, looking for Amy when I saw her come out of the dining room, with tears in her eyes from laughing so hard. ("REDЯUM" spells "murder" backwards and was the famous line from the movie.)

We all had such a great time that night, and Amy never left! Lucky for me, my adopted parents never asked her to leave, which allowed me time to send a few more months with my sister before we lost our entire childhood.

While my sister is no longer married, I do have another memory that is special to me. While I was in college, I received a call from her, informing me she would be marrying her high school sweetheart the following month. *Finally,* I thought. They had been together for years! I desperately wanted to attend her wedding, but I didn't have the money to get there, as I was a broke college student. I was honest with my sister and told her I would try my hardest to show up, but there were no guarantees.

One afternoon, I told some friends my situation, and they insisted I go. Two of them even offered to drive me back to San Antonio, Texas. I was thrilled over their proposal, but I didn't want to tell my sister just in case something went wrong.

I kept the secret for the entire month leading up to her wedding. When the day finally arrived, my friends kept their word and drove me to my hometown. When we got to the church, I made sure to stay out of sight. It wasn't until my sister walked into the sanctuary and turned to walk down the aisle that she saw me. Her face lit up and from the back of the church, she yelled, "You came!" as she started crying.

While I say Amy is the one with the biggest heart out of all of us, I believe my sister Tammy is the strongest. The rest of my siblings and I have always joked that Tammy was the mean one, but what we didn't know then that we know now, was that my sister Tammy was being molested. She was abused until the age of 12 and became homeless at the age of 15, that is not a way to start life. I wouldn't blame my sister if she had chosen to be bitter for the rest of her life but what makes Tammy amazing is that she chooses to better.

For the longest time, my sister was a hospital advocate for the rape crisis center. Any time of day or night, if a young lady were sexually assaulted, my sister would rush to the hospital to be there with them before, during, and after the medical forensic examination. She did this because she didn't want them there alone. I could only imagine—each time my sister sat with a new victim—she would have to relive her own hell.

My sister had so much anger built up inside of her and didn't know how to release it healthily, she would often take it out on Amy and me. As we have gotten older, Tammy has learned to better control her anger. She is an avid reader of self-help books and always shares with us the latest book she's read to help us with our issues. Tammy is a good woman who is continuously working on herself... But what I've learned is not to piss her off or she'll release the Kraken!

When I was about 22 years old, Tammy and I became roommates. One night we sat at our kitchen table with a glass of wine and asked each other, "So, what happened to you?" referring to the time that we were separated during our teenage years.

We began to share our lives and experiences. I told my sister about all the homes I lived in, and she disclosed her own homeless story. She talked about the individuals who took her in, and when they no longer wanted her there, she would have to sleep outside. As her brother, that hurt to hear. The crazy thing is, her classmates would have never known the horrors she was facing. She was nominated for best dressed in school, but they weren't her clothes, she had borrowed them from her friends. Goes to show you never know another person's story.

While my older siblings and I had it hard, I think my little sister Danielle had it the worst. Amy, Tammy, Baby Ray, and I have some good childhood memories, but not Danielle. Her entire childhood was taken, and she would never get it back. From the time that she was 7 years old, she was surrounded by so many broken and toxic individuals, that she had no chance of a normal childhood. The violence in our home became increasingly frequent that everyone was trying to survive in their own way. While there were moments of joy in the life we come to adapt to, it wasn't the childhood Amy, Tammy, and I had.

By the age of 8 years old, Danielle had been passed around to so many people while we lived in hiding. She had seen our mother beaten many times and was so traumatized that the sound of a truck passing by would bring her to tears. She associated the sound with our father's truck and the violence that would occur each time he found us.

God, my heart breaks writing this. What's worse is our story isn't an isolated one, there are so many kids in this country dealing with the same issues.

Danielle had been broken by everyone who was supposed to love her, including me. I am embarrassed and ashamed to write this, but at that time, I loved to see my younger siblings cry. I think it was because I wanted to know someone was hurting just as bad as I was. I always hurt Danielle. I would hit her, pinch her, or make her think I was going to hurt her. I just wanted to instill fear in her. She became my outlet.

I told her, "This is how life works. I'm older, so I get to hurt you, and you get to hurt Baby Ray."

I was trying to justify to myself, that it was okay to make her cry. It wasn't until I was older that I apologized to both of them and admitted that I was wrong. It was not okay for me to hurt them, but the damage had been done. It's not surprising to me that she couldn't think of a good childhood memory, and I hate myself for that.

I knew what we had done to her, all of us. My parents broke her, our older siblings left her, and I hurt her. Without knowing, in our brokenness, we stole her childhood and expected her to grow up to be a well behaved, functioning adult.

One night, my mother and two older sisters were standing in the kitchen, and the topic of conversation was Danielle. My sisters couldn't believe the decisions she had been making. After a few minutes of listening to them gossip about how stupid her decisions and actions were I couldn't take it anymore. I finally jumped in the conversation and asked, "Well, what do you expect from her? This is what we ALL have taught her. Mom, you taught her it's okay to live with a man without being married. Amy, you taught her to support a man who can't keep a job. Tammy, you taught her to have a child out of wedlock, and I taught her that partying is great. I glamorized it, but what I didn't teach her was how horrible the hangovers were the next morning or how many jobs I've gone through this year because I keep getting fired. We can stand here and talk about Danielle, but she is just doing exactly what we've taught her. If we want her to change, then we have to change too."

My little sister was a product of her environment, but just because we grow up a certain way doesn't mean we have to stay in that mindset. Yes, we showed Danielle those negative behaviors, but it is up to each of us to decide if we want to remain in an unhealthy mindset. As we become adults, we can't blame our parents, family, or our past for how we choose to live our life. There comes a time when we all have to grow up and take personal responsibility for our behaviors and actions. We have to create the life we want.

My little sister has struggled to find her voice and place in life. She has had to unlearn so many of the horrible lessons we taught her. However, I am thankful that she is working hard to become a better mother, partner, daughter, and sibling.

Danielle has grown to be a beautiful young lady inside and out. Yes, she deals with her demons, but we all do. She is well on her way in life and was the first one out of our siblings to purchase her own home.

She said, "Roy, there are times I drive the girls (my nieces) to some of the houses we were in hiding, and I tell them everything we went through. I then promise them, they will never have to live the life mommy lived."

All my siblings are amazing in their own way, and we are all close. I think it's because we know what it feels like to be torn apart, but now that we have each other, we aren't going to let each other go. When we see one of our siblings straying away from the family or a healthy lifestyle, we have what we call a "sibling intervention." We get together, discuss the issue at hand, and develop a game plan. Then, we approach the troubled sibling and in love share our concerns but give the support that is needed to help our sibling weather their storm.

Our baby brother is everyone's pride and joy. I can't believe I actually put that in writing, but whatever. Baby Ray has had the most stable childhood out of all of us, but I believe it was the loneliest. Growing up, we all had each other, but Baby Ray was alone for the most part. When he was finally back to living with my mother and stepfather, he had no siblings there to entertain him, as we had all moved on. Even though we tried to be there for him, our absence was evident.

I recall coming home from college one time and taking him to a movie. I said to him, "From now on, when I'm home, I will take you to a movie and you can choose whichever movie you like." His eyes got so big.

As we got to the theater, I purchased our tickets, and we made our way in. I headed to the concession stands and told my baby brother, "You can get whatever you want."

Baby Ray stood there looking at the possibilities. After a few minutes, believe it or not, he found a candy that was on sale for only fifty cents.

He pointed at the candy and said, "I want that one."

I knew my little brother didn't *want* that one, I didn't even want that one. I said, "Mijo, you can get whatever you want."

He reassured me, "I want that candy."

At that moment, I realized what he was doing. I recognized the pattern. My little brother didn't want the candy that was on sale, but he feared he would be a burden if he asked for anything else. He may have even thought, *If I am a burden, then my brother may never bring me back again.* I knew his pain because I felt the same way each time I moved into someone's house. I needed to quickly become invisible so that I could stay longer. My little brother was trying to be invisible.

I kneeled down in front of him and said, "Ray, let me explain something to you. You have a voice and your voice matters. I never want you to be scared of using it because if you are, that's going to affect every aspect of your life. It will affect your relationships, and it will affect your career. I need to know what *you* want, don't be scared to tell me. I promise I will bring you back. However, I want you to understand something."

My little brother put his head down, thinking he was in trouble.

"Mijo, look at me, you're not in trouble. Ray, I love you, and I want to get you what you want but understand this; if I can't afford to get you something, that doesn't mean I don't love you. It means I can't afford it, but never be scared to use your voice. Mijo, share with me what you want."

A tiny smile came across his face.

"You understand that I love you, right?"

He nodded his head enthusiastically.

"Okay, let's practice using your voice," As I asked him once again, "Mijo, what would you like?"

With a big smile, he said, "I would like nachos, popcorn, candy, and a Coke."

I said, "You got it!"

I bought my little brother his treats, and we walked in and enjoyed our movie.

I must remind myself to be a brother and not a mentor when it comes to Baby Ray. I want so much for him that I am always giving him advice and trying to correct him. I must learn that it's okay to just be his brother.

I know I focus a lot on my biological siblings because that's who I have the most memories with, but, as I mentioned, family is the love that is in your heart, not the blood that flows through your veins. I am beyond blessed to have my stepsister, Joy, who has been there for me in many ways. While I may not be close to all my step-siblings, primarily because I don't live in Texas and travel constantly, I do feel a significant connection to Joy, and I want her to know I love her very much. I know she thinks I am absolutely nuts and she's right, but I love her dearly.

I remember being on the tour and one Christmas, I received a card from her. When I opened it, it was a $100 gift card. I knew she was a single mother, so this gift was even more significant. I hope and pray that I am just as good of a step-brother and she feels the love I have for her.

While attending Northwest Vista Community College, I was working at a family owned, hole in the wall, Mexican restaurant named Los Chiles Verdes. The owners, Mr. and Mrs. Pete Pruneda, were more than just my bosses, they were my friends. I don't think they fully understood my background or what I had gone through, but their generosity was incredible. Many nights, I would go into the restaurant, even if wasn't scheduled to work. I just went to hang out with them because I loved staying after hours talking about life. I was so hungry for a better life that I absorbed every word they said. I think what I loved most was their family. They had something I dreamed of and talking to them gave me hope.

During my time at NVC, I also held a work-study position, but during lunch I would rush to Los Chiles Verdes and work the register. This would allow me a hot meal and to see my restaurant family. After lunch, I rushed back to campus to finish my classes for the day, then returned again to work the night shift.

When I enrolled at NVC in San Antonio, I wasn't in a healthy place in life. I had just moved out of my adopted parents' house, and I was forced to look in the mirror and try to figure out who I was as a young adult. I no longer had to conform to anyone's ideas of who Roy should be just so I could have a roof over my head. It was just me. I became self-destructive and started drinking excessively. My life was spiraling out of control and I was about to get kicked out of college.

One day, when I got to work, the Dean of Students at that time—Debi Gaitan—came into our office looking for me. I thought I was in big trouble, but she said, "Roy, will you be coming to the Yo Soy El Army event this afternoon? I would love for you to introduce our special guest."

"Sure, who is it?" I asked.

"Her name is Retired Lieutenant Colonel Consuelo Castillo Kickbusch."

At that moment, my heart stopped because I knew who this woman was. She was the same woman who 7 years earlier was speaking at the hotel I had snuck into. She was the one who had inspired me to get my little brother and go back to high school.

"I would love to introduce her!" I replied.

No one on campus knew about my story, because I was taught at a young age, what happens at home, stays at home. What that lesson teaches a kid is to be silent, it teaches you to not use your voice. I decided to break tradition and told it all.

That afternoon, in front of the dean, my bosses, the Army, and my peers, I introduced Colonel Kickbusch as a woman who gave me a second chance at life and never even knew it. I looked over to where she was standing and said, "You don't know me ma'am, but we've met before." You could see a look come over the dean's face, probably thinking, *what is he talking about?*

I continued, "Seven years ago I snuck into a hotel as a homeless teenager just to steal a meal, but that night you gave me something more. Ma'am, you gave me hope. Today I am in college because of you."

There wasn't a dry eye in the room.

Two weeks after that event, I received a call from her office asking if I would come to speak at her book signing. I accepted the offer. Two weeks after that, they called me again and offered me a three-month internship that lasted two years. During that time, Mrs. Kickbusch kept telling me, "Roy, you have to share your story. There are a lot of hurting kids who need you."

I decided I would give it a try, but before I did, I had to talk to my mom and step-dad.

I invited my parents to Los Chile Verdes for dinner. When they arrived, I greeted them both. As we sat in that little Mexican restaurant, I began sharing my life with them, my truth. We all sat and cried as I told them everything I had planned on saying in my presentations. Afterward, they were both apologetic.

They said, "Roy, we are so sorry. We never intended to hurt you. You always seemed so strong, like you had everything together. We're so sorry."

"I didn't come here for an apology, I thank you for it, but that's not what I was seeking. I just wanted you to hear from me what I am going to say. I don't want to hurt either one of you. I wanted you to hear it from me first."

I love my mom and stepdad. Honestly, I don't think I would have a mom if it weren't for him. I think she would have committed suicide from being so hurt and broken. He was the backbone that she needed to survive, and I will forever be grateful to him for that. He is a good man. Has he made mistakes? Of course, but we all do. It's important to make it right, and he has. I love that man with all my heart, and I know my siblings do too.

As for my mother, words can't even describe my love for her. She is my one and only. Yes, I have other moms, an adopted and mentor mom, but my mother will always have my heart. She was God's gift to me, and I am eternally grateful for her.

## Our Journey Continues...

THANK YOU FOR taking the time to learn about my pilgrimage on the Homeless by Choice Tour. It changed the entire course of my life and opened my eyes to the issues our youth face. I hope this snapshot of my experience inspired and motivated you in some way.

To learn more about my work or find out when my next book will be released, connect with me!

www.HomelessbyChoice.com

www.LinkedIn.com/in/RoyJuarezJr
www.Facebook.com/RoyJuarezJr
www.Instagram.com/RoyJuarezJr
www.YouTube.com/RoyJuarezJr
www.Twitter.com/RoyJuarezJr